A GUIDE FOR NEW PLANNERS

1991 Edition

Donald M. Norris
and
Nick L. Poulton

The Society for College and University Planning

A GUIDE FOR NEW PLANNERS

ISBN 0-9601608-2-5

1991 Edition

Donald M. Norris
and
Nick L. Poulton

Published by:
Society for College and University Planning
339 East Liberty Street
Suite 300
Ann Arbor, Michigan 48104 USA
Phone 734.998.7832
Fax 734.998.6532
Email info@scup.org
www.scup.org

About the Authors

Donald M. Norris is president of Strategic Initiatives, Inc., a management consulting firm specializing in strategic planning, strategic marketing, and organizational assessment. The firm's clients include colleges and universities, major American and multinational corporations, associations, other nonprofit organizations, and government agencies. Prior to founding Strategic Initiatives, Inc., Dr. Norris was vice president and director of the Washington Office of the M&H Group, Inc. He previously was director of policy and management services at Advanced Technology, Inc., a Washington-area consulting firm. Dr. Norris served as a planner and institutional researcher in institutions of higher education for over twelve years, as director of planning and policy analysis at the University of Houston – University Park and in a variety of administrative posts at the University of Texas at Austin, the Universtiy of Michigan, and Virginia Polytechnic Institute and State University. He is a well-known author on a variety of topics relating to strategic planning, new university models in metropolitan areas, and enrollment management. Most recently, he authored *Market Driven Management: Lessons Learned from Twenty Successful Associations*. Dr. Norris holds a B. S. in Engineering Mechanics, an M. B. A. from Virginia Polytechnic Institute and State University, and a Ph. D. from the Center for the Study of Higher Education at the University of Michigan.

Nick L. Poulton is a senior consultant with Strategic Initiatives, Inc. He is chief administrative officer for a US AID-funded project running the Midwest University Consortium for International Education (MUCIE) in Pakistan. Dr. Poulton has served with a variety of consulting firms in the Washington area specializing in information resource management and strategic planning. Prior to that, he was director of planning and development at the University of the South Pacific, where he was responsible for planning and negotiating resources from over twenty government and international agencies. Dr. Poulton's twenty-five years experience in higher education also includes university planning at Western Michigan University, academic planning and analysis at the University of Michigan, and engineering technology education at Purdue University, both in the United States and in Afghanistan with a U.S.-funded engineering program. He holds a B. S. and M. S. in Electrical Engineering from Purdue University and a Ph. D. from the Center for the Study of Higher Education at the University of Michigan.

Acknowledgements

Any work such as this owes a special debt to the many authors in the field of planning whose works are summarized and annotated in *A Guide for New Planners*. Culminating in this third edition, *A Guide for New Planners* has benefited from helpful comments from Michael Dolence, Marvin Peterson, George Keller, Reynolds Ferrante, David Dill, R. Sue Mims, Frank Schmidtlein, and Edward Delaney, to whom we express our appreciation. Reccommendations on short lists of key current references in the tactical planning areas were provided by Frank Schmidtlein, Larry Leslie, Robert Barak, Bernie Sheehan, Ray Zammuto, and Kim Cameron. O. Robert Simha provided some useful citations and ideas in the area of facilities planning.

Finally, it is a pleasure to acknowledge the membership of the Society for College and University Planning, who, by requesting an up-to-date guide for planners, have made this revised edition possible. The authors wish to express special thanks to the Publications Committee headed by Haskin Pounds, the Board of the Society for College and University Planning for their support in commissioning this document, and to Joanne MacRae and Connie Taylor for their assistance and suggestions.

Table of Contents

List of Exhibits

1

Introduction to Planning: Getting Started

So You Have Been Asked to Plan?

Most college and university planners remember well the circumstances that led them to become associated with their institution's planning activities. While the chain of events varies from setting to setting, generally the episode went something like one of these:

- You have just been hired as director of planning at a regional state university reporting directly to the president. By creating this new position, your president has made a commitment to planning and also has expressed a feeling that serious planning has not yet occurred at the institution. On arriving, you find you have no real job description and no real directions other than "to plan."

- As vice president for administration, you have been asked by the president to recommend a process of dealing with the potential implications of your newest telecommunication proposal for the academic, administrative, financial, and physical facilities components of the campus. The president also wants you to consider its implications for interacting with off-campus learning centers and constituencies. Your proposal deals solely with the technical aspects of several alternatives for wiring the campus, and you are uncertain of how to proceed.

- Your state has experienced a severe budgetary crisis as a result of the recent economic downturn. Your institution has been instructed to prepare for a two percent immediate reduction in this year's budget, to be effective by mid-year, and another five percent reduction next year. Your president has instructed the provost and you, the vice president for planning and budget, to plan for both sets of reductions, but by the second year to couple budget reduction with a serious scrutiny of administrative processes and academic services.

- While there is an existing planning process at your college, your

1

president has charged you with injecting that process with a strategic-planning flavor. Environmental scanning and issues management have been mentioned as possible methodologies, but the president has given no further guidance on how to incorporate them into the existing fabric of planning, saying, "You're the executive assistant to the president. You tell me!"

- As vice president for academic affairs at a small liberal arts college, you are concerned about the program mix at your institution and your ability to deal with the increasingly technological interests of many students and the need to "internationalize" your curriculum. After receiving considerable pressure from the board to make the college's program more relevant, your president has asked you to develop an action plan specifying potential changes in your academic program.

- As vice president for research, you have decided to review the university's research park and incubator programs, which have been modestly successful as real estate ventures but have not achieved their potential linkages with academic and research programs at your university. A new vice president for academic affairs has been chosen, replacing a person who was uninterested in either program. The president is supportive of your efforts, but has some notions of the potential for these ventures which may not agree with your assessment of the best way to proceed.

- As director of facilities planning at a major research university, you have just received a copy of a memo from the vice chancellor for academic affairs, complaining that planning for the new natural sciences building has failed to recognize many of the needs of other disciplines and the long-term academic goals of the campus. You had utilized a planning committee in support of this project, but it was not connected with university-wide planning activities. You have now been instructed to propose changes in the structure of the planning process to ensure that this problem does not happen again.

- In your newly appointed role as director of institutional research, you are expected to provide analytical support for the planning process, which is scheduled to begin its new cycle next month. The type of data provided in the last cycle was generally regarded as being too detailed and poorly structured, but you have not specifically been asked to revise the format.

- Based on an idea picked up at a professional conference, the president of your community college has directed you, in your capacity as director of admissions and records, to form an "enrollment management council" not only to orchestrate recruiting and retention efforts and enrollment services, but also to deal with the challenges posed by increasing numbers of minority and older students. In the past, these functions have been performed by different committees reporting to different vice presidents. You are to have the committee in place and functioning within a month.

- As vice chancellor of academic affairs at a growing, comprehensive university in a booming, "hypergrowth" metropolitan area, you are attempting to make some sense of requests from three new "urban villages" for substantially enhanced academic offerings—especially master's-level offerings for young engineers and other professionals—at locations in their communities. Your president is supportive, but the state is short of resources and many state leaders support development at the upstate, research universities. Your president wants you to convene a working group of campus and community leaders to fashion and recommend a strategy for proceeding.

- Your state's coordinating board has just launched a comprehensive, blue ribbon task force for a review of quality in higher education, and you have been designated as the official representative from your university to the faculty advisory committee supporting the task force. Your first meeting is next week, and you have been asked to submit to your president a strategy for dealing with the situation.

- In your capacity as executive assistant to the president, you have been instructed to work with administrative and academic units, to help them develop their capacity to plan more effectively. The president is planning to place greater flexibility and responsibility down into the organization. Your role is to develop these units' capacities.

The common thread linking each of these situations is that someone or some group has been asked to plan or to play a role in support of a planning process. Or someone has come to understand that planning is important and is searching for a way to advance the cause of planning at his/her institution. Or perhaps a college reaccreditation team, a college executive committee, the leadership of a development/capital campaign, or some other group is attempting to use planning to fulfill its charge. Or a particular problem-solving opportunity enables the institution to both address the problem and to plan for a broader set of implications of the problem. The institutional settings are different, as are the nature of the problems and the characteristics of the actors or groups. Participants may include a variety of campus groups —and stakeholders from the community, industry, and political groups, as well. But in each case, some individuals or group has been called upon to design and implement planning, generally with insufficient or even poor guidance, and under less than optimum conditions.

The purpose of this monograph is to help the planner to plan under such circumstances. Chances are, you are beginning to plan in a similar situation.

But you are not alone. Planning seldom begins under textbook conditions; it almost never proceeds with perfect precision. Sometimes the planner receiving no guidance at all is more fortunate than the planner receiving guidance that is poorly conceived or misdirected. The purpose of this monograph is to help the new planner learn from the experiences of other planners about how to launch—and how not to launch—successful planning processes.

This is not a cookbook on how to plan by the numbers. So-called "prescriptive planning models"—those that assume perfectly rational decision making and pay inadequate attention to uncertainty and differences in environments—suggest ironclad steps and conditions for planning, but our approach does not. Rather, this is a *roadmap* of the field of planning that will help the planner to survey the situation and to develop a strategy for planning. Good planning is more an art than a science in that it depends on sage assessment and careful implementation based on the uniqueness of particular situations. Our roadmap suggests factors one should consider and where one can go in the literature to find assistance in formulating questions and developing answers.

Another way to make this point is to use Harold Enarson's apt metaphor, which distinguishes between the "Cook's Tour" approach to planning and the "Lewis and Clark" model. The Cook's Tour defines a precise schedule on a well-defined route; it moves in orderly progression past known landmarks. Its aim is to avoid contingencies and the unknown and to structure planning in a scheduled, ordered, and routine manner. On the other hand, the Lewis and Clark model incorporates a sense of adventure in the exploration of new planning frontiers. Lewis and Clark had a clear sense of context, direction, and what to look for, but their actual course was unknown. The Cook's Tour model gives the false impression of stability, while the Lewis and Clark model suggests values and principles that can help the planner to deal with the uncertainty and unpredictability of planning. Clearly, the Lewis and Clark model best suits higher education planning.

This monograph begins by describing certain characteristics and components of planning that the planner must understand and by recommending actions that the new planner should avoid until he/she has analyzed the situation and determined what initiatives are appropriate. It then suggests a framework that the planner should utilize in analyzing the new planning environment, the potentials of his role, the particular institutional needs, and the type of planning activities which are appropriate. It also provides an analysis of how planning has changed over the years and how the planner must reinterpret the literature and theory of planning based on emerging issues, new challenges, and new techniques; this is critical to using the reference bibliography on the field of planning that is provided. This guide also suggests the several references and critical resources in each of several topical areas that are critical to developing understanding and to broadening competence for the new planner.

Understand the Characteristics of Planning and of Successful Planners

However you decide that planning is necessary, either by directive, by appointment to a planning committee, or by responding to a problem that needs solving, you must understand some basic characteristics of planning. Moreover, you should also know what separates successful planners from those who labor with one planning process and then move on to other fields of endeavor. Exhibit 1 summarizes the characteristics of planning and of successful planners and the relationship of planning to other organizational functions.

Characteristics of Planning

Several attributes are common to all planning activities. First, planning should occur at all levels of the organization. Planning behavior is a basic responsibility of all managers, administrators, and academic leaders, and whether or not one is called a planner, planning is necessary to deal with the challenges of operation. In addition, planning can range in complexity and scope from simple problem-solving activities to complex strategic planning or to comprehensive, long-range planning. Even if you are the only administrator with the word "planning" in your title, you are certainly not the only planner at your institution. Indeed, most so-called university planners are truly support staff to planning processes, while the true planners are faculty and administrators with "line" responsibilities.

Second, even if you are the first person in your organization officially to be designated with planning in your title, you are certainly not the first planner in your organization. Nor will you be the last. You must be aware of the strengths, weaknesses, and percep-

Exhibit 1:
The Characteristics of Planning and Successful Planners

Characteristics of Planning:

- Planning is a basic responsibility of all leaders and managers. It should occur at all levels of the organization.
- You are neither the first nor the last planner in your organization.
- Planners should encourage "planning oriented behavior" on the part of institutional citizens.
- Planning must pay attention to the timeframes, cycles, and sequences of institutional life.

Characteristics of Successful Planners:

Successful Planners:
- Are students of planning theory and practice;
- Are practical; they are insightful interpreters of their organization and its needs;
- Understand the role of different stakeholders in the outcomes of planning;
- Continually evaluate, assess, and rethink their planning efforts;
- Recognize the need to "plan for planning;"
- Are cognizant of the fact that sound implementation is key to successful planning.

Relationship of Planning to Other Organization Functions:

Planning is not superior to other management functions; it is one of the basic management functions – along with academic program development, marketing, fund raising, resource allocation, and program evaluation – which are the fundamental management tools of the institution.

tions of previous planning activities, both formal and informal. You must devise a strategy for dealing with this residue in constructing your current and future planning activities. Moreover, you should remember that what you are doing will provide the basis for the planning activities of whoever succeeds you. No matter how good your planning procedures are, they will be changed, and probably with good reason. Neither plans nor planning processes are carved in stone.

Third, regardless of your level and responsibility for planning, an important task for you is to encourage "planning-oriented behavior" both in your domain and in those with whom you associate. Planning-oriented behavior is a way of functioning and viewing the world that believes in the value of planning. It supports analytic approaches—not exclusively quantitative in nature—and aims at influencing and making decisions in the real world, not in a dream world of perfectly rational, apolitical decisions. By fostering planning-oriented behavior, you will support the growth of planning in your organization.

Fourth, planning must pay attention to the timeframes, cycles, and sequences of institutional life. If not carefully related, the timeframes of planning and institutional decision making can become hopelessly disjointed. The budget cycle operates as a common linking element for budgetary and financial planning at different levels, but somehow planning involving academic, financial, physical, and human resource components must be linked and integrated carefully if effective planning is to occur.

Characteristics of Successful Planners

A Guide for New Planners makes several critical assumptions about the characteristics of successful planners. First, successful planners are students of planning theory and practice; they study and understand the basic theories of planning and new developments in the field. Second, successful planners are practical and are insightful interpreters of their organization and its needs. They apply planning theory and techniques with a keen eye to the needs of their organization and with a sensitivity to the importance of political and organizational considerations in planning. They integrate thought and action exceptionally well and conduct both simultaneously. Third, they understand that the outcomes of planning affect a wide range of stakeholders—faculty, students, administrators, alumni, external publics—and that all of them have an interest in the planning process. These stakeholders are becoming more numerous and their interests more complex. Fourth, successful planners are continually evaluating, assessing, and rethinking their planning efforts.

Fifth, successful planners recognize the need to "plan for planning" and to assure the continued vitality of planning in their organization. Sixth, successful planners realize that the "proof of planning is in the implementation," and they emphasize the importance of sound and effective implementation techniques. *A Guide for New Planners* is structured to provide the tools necessary for both new and experienced planners to attain these characteristics and to maximize their success.

Relationship of Planning to Other Organizational Functions

It is critical for the successful planner to understand the relationship of planning to other management functions of the organization. Planning is but one of the institution's basic management functions, along with academic program development and management, resource allocation, fund raising, evaluation of academic and administrative programs, marketing and enrollment management, and others. These managerial functions are part of the ongoing responsibilities of line managers, who often are assisted by special support staffs for these functions. Planning is often an instrument through which leadership confronts or deals with these other managerial functions, but planning is not superior to the other organizational functions. The successful planner must understand the relationship between these functions and craft planning activities to enhance the effectiveness of these other managerial activities.

Effective planning makes all of the management functions more effective. And the insights gained from successfully utilizing the full range of academic management skills strengthens the planning processes in the academic and administrative units and in the institution as a whole.

Understand the Different Types of Planning

It is important to understand the definitions, characteristics, and strengths of different types of planning. For example, *strategic planning* is the activity through which one confronts the major strategic decisions facing the organization. A decision is not rendered strategic merely by being important. By Robert Shirley's definition, strategic decisions or issues fulfill the following criteria:

- Define the institution's relationship to its environment
- Generally take the whole organization as the unit of analysis
- Depend on inputs from a variety of functional areas
- Provide direction for, and constraints on, administrative and operational activities throughout the institution

Strategic planning is performed on an irregular timeframe as strategic challenges emerge. Strategic planning has grown in popularity in higher education as educational leaders adopt a more proactive, external orientation.

Some planners make the distinction between strategic planning and other types of planning: long range, tactical, and operational. A common characteristic of these types of organizational planning is that their timeframes and cadences are defined by the needs of the organization, not by a changing environment. *Long-range planning* is a more routine and regular type of planning that operates within the guidelines set by strategic planning, on a five-to-ten-year horizon. On the other hand, *tactical planning* consists of the short-term or intermediate-term, regular planning and budgeting activities dealing with administrative and operational activities that unfold within the overall strategic context of objectives established by strategic planning. *Operational planning* deals with short-term activities, generally on a one-year timeframe, that translate tactical plans into annual implementation.

In some applications, operational planning is called problem-focused, contingency, or performance-improvement planning. *Problem-focused or contingency planning* is generally short term and highly focused, dealing with problems that exist today. The solutions to these problems may be achievable in the long term, but the activities are highly targeted to deal with current problems. The use of the term *performance improvement planning* alludes to the use of operational planning to tune and improve the performance of current operations through annual adjustment. While each of these terms characterizes operational planning with a slightly different nuance of meaning, each is consistent in viewing operational planning as a practical, immediate, short-term activity having concrete results.

It is possible, however, to use the opportunity afforded by addressing a problem to engage in strategic planning. For example, an institution can respond to an outdated mission statement by engaging in strategic thinking and generating a new mission statement. Or a president can use a programmatic crisis as the occasion for seriously reexamining institutional programs. Indeed, most good strategic thinking that occurs in universities is catalyzed by a particular problem that provides a window for examining the university's strategic opportunities and challenges. So problem-focused planning can be strategic as well as operational.

Robert Shirley has devised an especially helpful typology for dealing with strategic planning in the college or university. His "four levels of strategy" recognize that strategy is dealt with not only at the institutional level, but by colleges, departments, and other subunits. *Level 1: Institutional Strategy* deals with matching environmental opportunities with internal strengths to determine basic mission, clientele, goals, program/service mix, geographic service area, and comparative advantage. *Level 2: Campus-wide Functional Strategies* deal with plans for finances, enrollment, admissions and recruitment, human resources, organization, and facilities to achieve the strategies outlined in the first level. *Level 3: Program Strategies* are plans by academic units in response to Levels 1 and 2, setting strategic profiles, action priorities, and resource requirements. *Level 4: Program-level Function Strategies* are the plans for admissions, curriculum, staffing, recruitment, and budget to achieve the program strategies established in Level 3. This typology shows how strategy at the institutional level gets translated into strategy and into tactical and operational plans at the program level.

One must note that strategy moves up as well as down the organization. Under Shirley's levels 3 and 4, departments often craft their own strategies and visions. They initiate as well as respond, especially in the absence of well-articulated institutional strategies.

None of these typologies of planning is intrinsically superior to the other. In any setting, all types of planning must occur, but in different measure, depending on the nature of the environmental challenges facing the organization, the nature of the organization, and a variety of situational factors. While strategic planning is enjoying growing popularity in higher education, it has not eclipsed the more traditional focus of long-range, tactical, and operational planning, which must still continue in the organization.

Linking Strategic and Organizational Planning

Consequently, one of the critical understandings for today's planner is how to link strategic-planning activities with the more traditional organizational planning activities. Exhibit 2 illustrates the differences between strategic and organizational planning and suggests means to link strategic and organizational planning. Strategic planning is externally directed, focuses on "what" the organization should do, deals with "macro" issues, spans organizational boundaries, is a continuing process dictated by changes in the environment that occur on an irregular timeframe, deals with relatively greater levels of uncertainty, and values expert judgment. Organizational planning is internally focused, emphasizes "how" to do the "what" stipulated by strategic planning, deals with the impact of macro issues on micro issues, is tied to organizational units and the budget/resource allocations process, is relatively certain—or at least

Exhibit 2:
Distinguishing Between Strategic Planning and Other Types of Organizational Planning

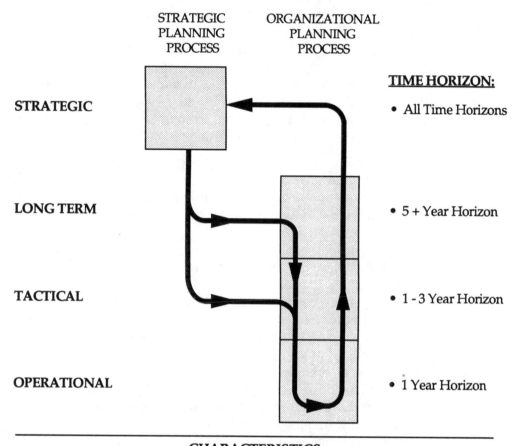

STRATEGIC
PLANNING
PROCESS

ORGANIZATIONAL
PLANNING
PROCESS

STRATEGIC

LONG TERM

TACTICAL

OPERATIONAL

TIME HORIZON:

- All Time Horizons

- 5 + Year Horizon

- 1 - 3 Year Horizon

- 1 Year Horizon

CHARACTERISTICS:

STRATEGIC	ORGANIZATIONAL
• External Focus	• Internal Focus
• What To Do	• How To Do It
• Macro Issues	• Impact of Macro Issues on Micro Issues
• Boundary Spanning	• Tied to Organizational Units
• Continual Scanning Process to Notice Changes Occuring Irregularly, Dictated by Environment	• Regular Processes Dictated by Organizational Cycles
	• Linked to Budget/Resource Allocation Process
• Expert Participation	• Constituent Participation

depends on the appearance of certainty—and is highly participatory and constituency based. It is often necessary to craft an entirely different planning process and structure to deal with strategic planning, but to link them with the existing processes and structures for organizational planning.

One of the most tantalizing features of Exhibit 2 is the arrows linking strategic planning with organizational planning. A whole monograph could be written on how to make these linkages work in different settings. There is no single tool or methodology that will work in every setting; however, combinations of the following items, which are summarized in Exhibit 3, offer several possibilities:

- Use small, cross-disciplinary work groups to generate strategies and implications for implementation. Excellent strategic thinking is best conducted by your best strategic thinkers, consulting with a wide variety of sources, but utilizing their own strategic judgment.
- Use environmental scanning to search out the emerging issues and challenges that require changes in strategy. The information and insight gathered and analyzed through environmental scanning can assist the institution as a whole, and individual units, in their planning. Let the environmental scanner beware, however; overly formalized and routinized processes can bog down the planning process.
- Use the techniques of issues management to translate those macro changes into impacts on micro components of tactical and operational planning. Convert environmental-scanning insights into easily understood expressions of their impact on tactical and operational planning. Issues management is useful both in support of strategic thinking and during tactical planning/ implementation.
- Generate a simple, clear "vision of the organization of the future." This statement should describe what the future organization will look like and how it will function. This vision statement is a useful guide to the tactical planning and implementation as a focal point for change when new strategies emerge. However, a note of warning: this can be among the most potentially controversial component of planning. Sometimes ambiguity is a virtue!
- Demonstrate a willingness to modify and tinker with established plans as new strategies emerge. "Plans," "strategic vision," and other products must be flexible and revised as conditions change.
- Provide a clear statement of strategic vision and the impact of

strategies on different stakeholders. This task can be difficult. Sometimes it is best to utilize trial balloons to test stakeholder opinion.

- Have a strategic-thinking group review summaries of tactical plans for consonance with institutional strategies.

These are all components of successful linkages between strategic thinking and organizational planning. If you recognize the differences between strategic and organizational planning, and accommodate those differences in the design of your planning processes, you can successfully conduct both strategic planning and organizational planning. If you fail to recognize these differences and attempt to "shoehorn" strategic planning into an organizational planning process, the results will be unsatisfactory.

Universities are not the only organizations facing the conflict between strategic and organizational planning. In his book, *The Mind of the Strategist*, Kenichi Ohmae observes that the extent and quality of true strategic thinking in an organization is inversely proportional to the amount of formal analysis and planning in the organization! In other words, no matter what you call organizational planning, it tends to stifle true strategic thinking. So one is best served by designing processes that separate strategic and operational planning, then link the results.

In the 1990s, many universities—both public and private—will have ample opportunities to link strategic thinking with operational planning. Many are facing the need to reexamine their mission, values, and means of academic delivery and administrative support services. In many settings, financial exigencies, internal pressures to seek a new paradigm for the university, and external pressures to reform the undergraduate curriculum and contain costs are providing challenging opportunities for strategic thinking. Often, these opportunities involve using a specific, problem-solving requirement—such as the need to trim and balance next year's budget—as a vehicle for strategically assessing the institution's approach to delivery of instruction, research, and public service. More discussion of the particular changes of the 1990s—and their impacts on planning—will follow in Chapter 4.

Numerous authors have created a variety of typologies that characterize planning in different ways. The important point is that the planner understands how the types of planning vary and can apply a framework for differentiating among types of planning that are sensible for his setting and are easily communicated. The planner must be able to convey this sense of the differences in planning,

Exhibit 3:
Linking Strategic Thinking and Organizational Planning

- Utilize small, cross-disciplinary work groups to generate strategies and implications of strategies for implementation;

- Employ environmental scanning to search out the emerging issues and challenges that require changes in strategy;

- Use the techniques of "issues management" to translate "macro" changes into understandable impacts on "micro" components of tactical and operational planning;

- Generate a "vision of the organization of the future" that can be a guide to tactical planning and implementation as well as a focal point for change as new strategies emerge;

- Provide clear, understandable statements of strategic vision and impacts of strategies on different stakeholders;

- Demonstrate a willingness to tinker with established plans as new strategies emerge;

- Have strategic-thinking group review summaries of tactical plans for consonance with institutional strategies.

and all information relating to the process and products of planning, in jargon-free, simple, expository English.

Appreciate the Importance of all Components of Planning

It is also important to evaluate your role and the planning needs of your organization in the context of the different components of planning:

- Planning structure
- Planning process
- Information and analytic support of planning

Every planning activity is composed of some combination of these three components, and it is critical that you achieve a balance among the three that is congruent with the purposes of planning and the needs of your environment.

Most planners have strong feelings about *planning structure,* the infrastructure of planning committees and support staff, and *planning process,* the actual flow and substance of the planning activities. But several generalizations are in order. First, all organizations must achieve in their planning structure and process some balance between "top-down" and "bottom-up" planning. In educational organizations, the balance often swings toward a participatory, bottom-up approach, but the new planner needs to seek a balance appropriate to the given setting. Often the key is to identify those components of planning that need not be participatory and can be centrally directed, while subtly but firmly providing top-down direction and articulation to those areas where participation and consensus are critical, thus adhering to the spirit of the academic ethic of bottom-up planning and faculty participation. The emphasis on top-down or bottom-up is different for different issues. Second, and as previously stated, structures and processes must change and evolve, and one is well served by building that consideration into one's structure and process from the start.

Of the three components of planning, planning structure and planning process are the most highly situational and the components about which the fewest helpful generalizations can be drawn. The successful tailoring of a planning process and structure to a particular setting—probably more art than science—must be based on careful, structured, insightful analysis of the organizational setting, both past and present, and the potentials and limitation of planning. It is also dependent on careful and skillful implementation through which process and structure can be further tuned and modified, based on changing conditions or greater insight. Planning structure and process must be integrated with the decision making process so that planning can inform and shape decisions, not provide support or contradiction for decisions already made. The planning process and structure must continually be tuned to remain integrated with the changing decision-making patterns.

Experience proves that a common mistake is to make planning processes over-formalized, too rigid, and bureaucratic. This "organizational cost" of the process should be kept as low as possible if it is to be accepted for long.

Information and analytic support are often the stepchild of the planning process, an afterthought used to provide piles of data for planning committees to "chew on" while the planning process unfolds. Properly designed, however, a program of analytic support can provide key environmental intelligence, can manage and identify the issues confronting the organization, and can move the process along by focusing attention and forcing decisions at appropriate junctures. Analytic support can be provided by a variety of parties and should consist of both qualitative and quantitative components, tailored to the types of planning being undertaken. This is typically a task of institutional research offices, but not exclusively.

Since the increase in popularity of strategic planning, even greater attention has been paid to analytic support of planning. Strategic planning utilizes substantially different types of information than does organizational planning. Exhibit 4 compares and contrasts these differences. Strategic planning typically deals with external data, environmental scanning, issues management, and scenario-casting activities that are far more adventuresome; deal with greater uncertainty; examine institutional values; and venture farther afield than does organizational planning. But at some point, even these ventures in speculation must be tied to decisions and strategies that link to the present and to the existing organizations. One of the key roles of planning staff is to support both strategic and organizational planning and to assist in the necessary linking of the two.

Avoid the Deadly Sins of Reflexive Planning Behavior

In addition to conceptual and theoretical knowledge about planning, the successful planner must go forth armed with the practical knowledge about how to make planning work. As a complement to knowing what one should do to embark on planning, it is equally important to know what not to do. New planners, or presidents that appoint new planners, often respond by reflex to the beginning of a planning engagement. Avoid at all costs the following temptations, which are summarized in Exhibit 5:

1. *Do not attempt to implement, off the shelf, a planning process from another institution or from a textbook.* Prescriptive models for planning or processes that worked at other institutions and are outlined in planning handbooks are good places to turn for ideas, but they should not be applied without careful analysis and adaptation to your special needs and circumstances. Conditions that make an approach effective in one setting may not be present in your setting.

2. *Do not assume that all planning activities must be comprehensive, institution wide, and time consuming.* Successful, effective plan-

Exhibit 4:
Different Information for Different Types of Planning and Decision Making

	Strategic	Long Term/Tactical/Operational
Orientation	• External	• Internal
Nature of Information	• Uncertain	• Certain
	• Wide Ranging	• Established, Narrow Focus
	• Specified by Environmental Conditions	• Specified by Organizational Cycles
	• Qualitative, Value-Laden, and Political	• Relatively Rational and Quantitative
Information System Focus	• Intelligence	• Relatively Rational and Quantitative
	• Values	
	• Alternatives	
Decision Support	• Decision Support Systems for Semi-Structured or Understructured Decisions	• MIS to Support Structured and Semi-structured Decisions

ning can be highly targeted and problem focused. In some cases, a succession of plans dealing with different units is more effective than a single, grand plan. Planning does not need to be part of a formally constituted planning process, although it should dovetail with the formal planning process, if one exists. It can be as simple or complex, and as abrupt or time consuming, as needs demand. Even robust, all-encompassing planning processes begin modestly. In time, one can move toward comprehensiveness, if conditions warrant, building on success.

3. *Do not spend six months reading and thinking before you do anything.* It is often better to take half the time to do something

Exhibit 5:
Avoid The Deadly Sins of Reflexive Planning

- Do not attempt to implement, off the shelf, the planning process that worked so well at another institution with which you are familiar.

- Do not assume that all planning activities must be comprehensive, institution wide, and time consuming.

- Do not spend six months reading before you do anything.

- Do not form a planning committee as your first act.

- Do not dwell on information needs that will take a year to complete or fulfill before you can move the process forward, and do not use data as a "security blanket."

- Do not label what you are doing as something new, revolutionary, and wonderful.

- Do not characterize planning as being able to solve all of your problems.

- Do not overemphasize the importance of a final plan.

- Do not claim that planning can address all issues at once.

- Be careful about proclaiming that your planning process is the first step in an on-going planning process.

- Do not assume that long-term plans are strategic or that any important issue is strategic.

- Do not assume that planning addresses only problem-solving needs.

- Do not encourage others to think of you as "The Institutional Planner."

eighty percent as well than to strive for perfection. Just as it is wrong to attempt to apply another institution's process off the shelf, it is equally wrong to attempt to study the problem to death. Precious opportunities will be missed, and a failure to generate planning products on a timely basis will erode what support planning has.

4. *Do not form a planning committee as your first act.* Many planning activities and processes at some point benefit from a formal planning committee, but the membership and charge of the committee must be carefully considered to meet the needs of your situation. Even worse than appointing the committee as your first action is inheriting a committee as part of your charge. It is best not to convene that committee before you have things for it to do or products to give it and before you have carefully structured the committee's role and limitations. Naming the committee may be your first *official* or *public* act, but it must come after deliberation. The committee membership should reflect the nature of the issue and what it will take to implement recommendations.

5. *Do not identify information needs that will take a year to complete or fulfill before you can move the process forward and do not use data as a "security blanket."* Information that is targeted to drive decisions is fine. Data gathered in a "surveillance mode" may keep you busy, but such data are not very useful. Build on information that is currently available; even if retooling will ultimately be necessary, do *not* redefine everything.

Two corollaries to this point are "Do not wait until all the information is in to move the process forward," and "Do not identify and start to collect the information needed before you have considered the questions to be asked." These roles may seem like pure common sense, but they are often ignored until it is too late.

6. *Do not label what you are doing as something new, revolutionary, and wonderful.* If you do not believe in truth in advertising at the beginning of your planning process, you will by the end. A corollary to this point is "Do not assume that planning is the only thing or even the most important thing going on in the life of your institution." Planning is one of many instruments that are being used to deal with the ongoing management responsibilities and functions of your institution.

7. *Do not characterize planning as being able to solve all of the institution's problems.* This is a further corollary of point #6. Even if decisions made by virtue of planning solve some of your problems, planning may actually help you to identify problems of which you were not aware and for which there are no easy answers. While university faculty and administrators generally don't slay the bearers of bad tidings, no patient appreci-

ates what will ultimately prove to be a good prescription while the taste of bad medicine is still lingering on the palate.

8. *Do not overemphasize the importance of a final plan.* In some cases, the process is as important as the plan, and the right decision resulting from the planning processes is more important than a library full of plans. Remember Eisenhower's dictum, "Plans are nothing, planning is everything." A plan may be necessary in your circumstances, but it may not be. Indeed, it is probably better to assume that a final plan of more than five pages is *not* necessary unless proven otherwise. The most important product of planning is the learning that takes place.

9. *Do not claim that a single planning process or effort can capture all issues.* In reality, planning that focuses on particular issues, placed in an appropriate context, is more successful than planning that tries to be all things to all issues. Planning processes need focal points and ways of separating the issues and devoting energies to the most important. Work with feasible, manageable tasks. Focus on a limited number of themes for each planning cycle.

10. *Be careful about proclaiming that your planning process is the first step (or second, or third, for that matter) in an ongoing planning process.* Don't get us wrong: continuity is critical, and many planning processes suffer from lack of integration among successive planning efforts. For existing planning processes, it is important that current and future planning will build on the lessons from past planning. For new planning processes, it is critical to suggest that future efforts will improve and that perfection is far from possible, initially. However, it is also possible to generate "anticipatory fatigue" if too much is made of the ongoing burden of planning in perpetuity.

11. *Do not assume that long-term plans are strategic or that any important issue is strategic.* Many organizations conclude that if they have a long-term plan dealing with important issues, they have done strategic planning. That conclusion is not necessarily true. The importance and timeframe of issues does not make them strategic. Strategic issues are those that deal with the organization's relationship with the environment and affect most of the organization. Thus all strategic issues are important, but not all important issues are strategic.

12. *Do not assume that planning addresses only problem-solving needs.* While it is true that to be successful, planning must deal with problems and be seen to provide at least some solutions, planning can deal with other needs as well. It can be a powerful instrument of organizational development and of political

orchestration. It can be used to build or divorce constituencies and political alliances. Planning can also be used to introduce ideas, concepts, and managerial approaches to the organizational community. Under some circumstances, these other uses of planning can be even more important than its problem-solving thrust.

13. *Do not encourage others to think of you as "the institutional planner."* Particularly if you are a staff member, being labeled as *the* planner is a liability. The naive will think you are making critical decisions (which could not be more wrong and could be dangerous if true), and those responsible may avoid their obligation to think strategically. The critical role is to entice line administrators and appropriate faculty members to exercise their responsibility to think strategically and plan for their respective units.

Now that we have addressed some basic concepts of planning and have identified some seductive traps that the planner must avoid, it is time to address what the planner should do when confronted with the challenge of a new planning engagement.

2

Moving Forward: Analyze, Act, and Analyze Some More

While knowing what *not* to do can help planners avoid costly mistakes, there is no clear-cut, prescribed sequence of what to do to launch planning. Using common sense and some of the principles that follow, the new planner can tailor a combination of thinking and action that suits her circumstances. It is critical that the planner thinks about what she is doing and plans for planning by following a structured, action-oriented agenda.

Think About Planning

One would not expect that college and university planners need to be told to think, but the lure of reflexive planning behavior is stronger than one might suspect. Even the experienced planner needs to refresh his thinking and discover new insights by reviewing recent work on planning. The new planner needs to draw more deeply on the literature, both old and new, to develop some basic understanding of the concepts and practices of planning. The purpose of the analysis of new trends in planning and of the bibliography on planning highlighted in *A Guide for New Planners* is to enable such research and analysis to be conducted expeditiously. While it is a grave error to research planning for six months before doing anything, it is an even more grievous error for an experienced planner not to review recent developments in the theory and practice of planning and not to organize his thoughts about planning before proceeding with his newest planning engagement. Just like in football, ballet, and public speaking, it never hurts in planning to revisit the basics.

While the literature on the theory and practice of planning is a good place to turn, the planner should also tap other sources, such as visits to other institutions and candid discussions with others involved in planning. Gathering "fugitive" documents and samples of planning materials—along with honest assessments of how they were received — will yield not just a prescriptive model that can be parroted, but also insights and ideas that can be reinterpreted in your own setting. Talking to administrators and faculty at your institution and others can generate some healthy input. Out of a comparative analysis of the experiences of others, filtered by an understanding of one's own institution, can come some helpful ideas and insights.

This analysis/research should enable the planner to develop a basic understanding of the following areas:

- Differences in the types of planning
- Variety in the components of planning
- New trends in planning
- Changing issues and challenges that drive planning

At the same time that you as a planner are researching and developing/ redeveloping your understanding of these topics, you should be analyzing the planning environment in which you will be operating.

Think About Your Planning Environment

There are several components of one's particular planning environment of which every planner should be aware:

- Your charge/mandate and your organization's challenges
- History of planning and resistance to planning
- Potentials for planning and limitations in planning

No matter how long you have been at your institution and no matter how many hours you have spent thinking about planning in the past, invest additional time before you begin each new planning engagement. Analyzing these institutional contextual factors can be time well spent.

Understand Your Charge/Mandate and Your Organization's Challenges

It is important to think before you act, but your analysis and reflections should not be focused so long as to delay timely action. Your first task should be to analyze the charge or mandate you have been given, or that you have requested, and determine whether it is definitive and/or binding. The limitations of a restrictive or poorly framed charge must be understood and to the extent possible, overcome. While most planners would prefer the luxury of collaborating with their president in drafting their charge, in real life they often must deal with a charge into which they had no input. The planner must also understand the nature of the challenges facing the organization, whether addressing all or any of these can be legitimately included in the charge, and how to confront these challenges through planning.

One of the key facts about planning is that it cannot be effective if it attempts to deal with too many issues at once. It is impossible to overemphasize this point. At any time, certain key issues or themes emerge, based on the nature of challenges facing the organization, the history of planning, and future changes in the environment that should be dealt with in today's planning process. Often a strategic-planning activity can be utilized to generate the themes that then serve as the context for the next round of organizational planning, or strategic planning can continue to generate new themes and issues as the organizational planning process proceeds along its prescribed path.

History of Decision Making and Planning/Resistance to Planning

In order to understand the potentials and limitations of planning, you must understand the history of decision making, planning, and governance at your institution or agency. In many cases, this analysis must extend to encompass a multi-institutional environment, either a system of institutions in which you operate, the public institutions in your state, or any other cluster of institutions of which you are a part. To understand the history of decision making and planning you must recognize the following:

- The style and context of your organization
- The usual structures and processes employed to make decisions in your organization
- The relative power of external and internal forces shaping decision making
- The nature and successes of planning in the past
- Any biases and prejudices against planning and their relative strength
- Key supporters and detractors of planning and governance and their power to obstruct the process

Planning must be integrated in the ongoing decision making and governance processes, and the planner must be wary of planning charges that ignore or attempt to finesse that issue. Sometimes new planning processes are created because of deficiencies in the existing decision making process; if they do not confront these problems directly, however, they are seen as dealing with symptoms rather than with the core problems. Furthermore, decision making cannot be suspended until a planning cycle has been completed. Problems and opportunities must continue to be faced and addressed as they arrive.

Understanding the history of planning is fundamental to success. Almost every planning process, no matter how successful, has its negative aspects. The "unsavory residue" from previous planning interactions can impede or destroy subsequent planning activities. Some experienced observers of institutional life believe that a key determinant of the successful planner is being able to walk through a previous planner's unsavory residue without getting any on the carpet.

It is too easy for believers in planning to underestimate both the resistance to planning in any organization and the resistance to your particular planning initiative. Don't be misled. Planners are prime targets for resistance, opposition, and second guessing. First, not everyone operates with the same notion of planning. For example, in most settings, academic affairs officers and financial officers can each make strong and cogent arguments that their brand of planning is best for the institution. Each will claim to include a place for strategic thinking, qualitative and quantitative judgments, academic values, and financial reality in his brand of planning. Each will truly believe that his variation is best for the organization, and depending on the circumstances, either may be right. Second, it is wrong to assume that resistance to planning is irrational or unjustified. Some institutional officers may feel they are better able to plan unfettered by the distractions of participatory planning processes, cumbersome review procedures, and protracted discussion. Others may consider strategic planning to be impractical crystal-ball gazing, and depending on the particular institutional history of planning and the issues at hand, they may be correct. Third, it is easy to underestimate the threat that planning poses in many traditional organizations. To the extent that it slices across hierarchical boundaries, planning can threaten existing power centers. It can also threaten to put planning staff and/or a planning committee between the president and the deans, vice president, and other officers. Defensive behavior to such a threat is neither irrational nor unwarranted.

It also is not always easy to determine what someone means when he says yes to planning. He may have a different vision of it than you do, or he may be jumping on the bandwagon to use your planning processes as a bully pulpit for showcasing his own pet issues and concerns, which may be antithetical to your own.

The adept student of planning must understand the nuances of the notion of "stakeholder" as it applies to his/her organization. On one hand, the supporters and detractors of the planning process are stakeholders who see the planning process itself as either a benefit or threat to their perspectives or interests. These stakeholders focus on the planning process as an instrument for enabling or controlling change and decision making. In addition, stakeholders, and others, have an interest in the outcomes of the planning process. They view certain outcomes or directives as supportive of, or antithetical to, their interests. Both groups of stakeholders will interpret your proposed planning process in the context of past planning activities at your institution.

Many a planning process that is otherwise well defined to meet the challenges facing the organization has been doomed by a failure to understand the lessons of organizational history and the inherent resistance to planning. Tactics for dealing with resistance in a politic manner are essential. Exhibit 6 summarizes how to understand the history of planning and potential resistance to planning.

Potentials and Limitations of Planning

As planners, we all believe in the potentials of planning. To establish balance, one must consider the limitations to planning and the obstacles to overcome in attempting to implement planning in higher education. Exhibit 7 cites several key limitations and obstacles that are especially restrictive on the application of planning in colleges and universities.

1. *Organizational goals in higher education are often vague and diffuse and even when well defined, are often contested.* Planning theory, as applied to most organizational settings, assumes that goals are clearly articulated and widely agreed upon. In higher education, goals are often purposely left vague and open to varying interpretation. When they are clearly stated, goals in higher education are often contested and even resisted. While in many cases it serves the planner better to define goals, in other cases it can serve the organization's planning purposes to leave the goals open to interpretation, at least initially.

2. *The division of responsibility is unclear for strategy setting between disciplinary units and the organization as a whole.* The strong disciplinary, decentralized nature of higher education makes strategy setting difficult for the organization as a whole. Individual units are scanning their own discipline's environment and are making informed micro judgments which may conflict with the macro judgments being made for the organization as a whole. On the other hand, individual units seldom consider adequately certain boundary-spanning issues and trends that may affect them in the future.

3. *Loose coupling of organizational units often precludes timely,*

Exhibit 6:
Understanding and Responding to Institutional Planning History and Potential Resistance

- Assess without prejudice any "unsavory residue" remaining from previous planning processes.

- Understand the threat that planning poses to existing institutional power bases.

- Identify key supporters and detractors of planning and their power to obstruct or strengthen planning.

- Be certain that the president supports your planning effort and makes his support known to leadership and the organization at large.

- Emphasize, by word and deed, that planning is a line function and planning support is a staff function.

- Work to build consensus and support.

- Do not oversell planning and keep an appropriate profile.

organization-wide responsiveness and setting of strategy. The disciplinary, decentralized orientation of colleges and universities is translated into strategy setting that is slower than one would consider optimal, because of the need for collaboration and verification. This fact must be recognized by the planner in establishing realistic timeframes and mechanisms for strategic response.

4. *Cultures and histories of universities often make them slow, if not hesitant, to change.* Colleges and universities have not survived for thousands of years by changing rapidly or dramatically — at least not often. Especially as regards basic values, colleges and universities are very stable. The faculty's orientation toward debate and review must be taken into account when assessing the potentials for change.

5. *Institutional leadership does not fully control the institution's direction.* In many cases institutional inertia or external forces are controlling organizational direction, and institutional leaders are managing or accommodating to those forces — in some cases

Exhibit 7:
Limtations To Planning and Obstacles To Overcome

- Organizational goals in higher education are often vague and diffuse and when well defined are often contested.

- The division of responsibility is unclear for strategy setting between disciplinary units and the organization as a whole.

- Loose coupling of organizational units often precludes timely, organization-wide responsiveness and setting of strategy.

- Cultures and histories of universities often make them hesitant to change.

- Institutional leadership does not necessarily control the institution's direction.

- There is seldom basic agreement on strategy; even if the institutional strategy is clear and well articulated, the strategy of individual units may not be clear and compatible with it.

- Institutional leadership may be poorly prepared, by training and experience, to set strategy.

- It is quite difficult to link value- and idea-oriented strategic planning to budget-oriented organizational planning.

---

because the external forces cannot be controlled or manipulated, but in other cases because of lack of leadership. To control the organization's direction, to the extent possible, leaders must lead.

6. *There is seldom basic agreement on strategy.* Just as there is disagreement in goals, there is wide variation of opinion on organizational strategy. Even among an apparently tightly knit leadership team, differences exist—and this is good.

7. *Even if institutional strategy is clear and well articulated, the strategy of individual units may not be clear and compatible with it.* This is a corollary to items #2 and #3. Indeed, there may be covert, but real, contradiction of organizational strategy in the intent and actions of individual units.

8. *Institutional leadership is sometimes poorly prepared, by training and experience, to set strategy.* Your organization's leadership may be adequately schooled in organizational planning but seriously deficient in setting strategy and performing strategic planning. The planner must recognize this and establish the education of leadership as a top priority, although it must be handled diplomatically and perhaps unobtrusively.

9. *It is difficult to link value-oriented and idea-oriented strategic planning to budget-oriented organizational planning.* One of the most common reasons for failures in strategic planning is the failure to link it adequately with organizational planning. The setting of "what to do" through common reasons for failures in strategic planning is the failure to link it adequately with organizational planning. The settng of what to do through strategic planning must be grounded in the reality of what levels of resources may be available. This factor, along with the high costs of planning, is the major reason for failure in many planning processes. Value-oriented strategy must be translated into operational terms that work for organizational planning.

Move Into Action: Launching Initial Activities

Concurrent with the analysis of planning needs, it is important to launch carefully considered and highly targeted planning activities. Continue to read in the planning literature to build on your foundation of understanding about the basic role and structure of planning and about the particular aspects which seem congruent with the problems facing your organization. But read critically; there is a good deal of bad advice in the literature! You should also develop an inventory of existing information sources, analytical capabilities, and planning tools. You must build upon this base, but not adhere slavishly to questionable practices. Develop a sense of what kinds of information are needed to support your mix of planning activities and how much of the existing information can be absorbed. At the same time, you can set in motion the process of fulfilling information requirements that are presently unfilled. But planning activities must move forward before all the information is completed.

Finally, possible participants in the planning process should be sought out, if they have not been already selected for you. The choice of participants should balance the need to represent certain constituencies with the need to choose persons who can be counted on to foster planning-oriented behavior. Select persons who have a stake in the issues under consideration and will see them through to action. While differences of opinion are generally healthy in moderate measures, persons of constructive, action-oriented demeanor are preferable to professional curmudgeons, pedants, congenital contemplators, and other sorts of "unplanners" who are lurking about, seeking the opportunity to become part of your planning process. A handful of unplanners can scuttle an otherwise well-conceived planning process. Unplanners thrive in academic environments and are easily recognizable by their behavior—avoid them like the plague.

In selecting small strategic-thinking groups, amplify this advice ten-fold. Seek your best thinkers, regardless of constituency. Select true planners who can relate future possibilities to current realities, but are not mired in the present.

Do not be afraid to change the structure, process, and analytical support of planning. Indeed, build flexibility into your process. As you continue to analyze your circumstances, your perception of needs will change. "Adapt or die" is an apt observation for planning processes, and one should engender both the expectations of change and the capability to change into one's planning activities. It is probably best to consider your structure/process/support design for planning as an "emergent design," providing enough structure and form to convince the planning publics that you know what you're doing, but maintaining enough flexibility to change process/structure/support to fit your emerging sense of what will succeed.

Analyze Some More

Having analyzed the environment for prospects for planning and having launched a number of planning-related activities, the planner should then devise a mixture of conscious tactics for each component of planning: the planning process, the formal planning structure, and the information and analytic support. Recognizing the particular needs and challenges of the situation, no two approaches to planning should be precisely alike. Take as an example an engineering department using planning to focus on its need to acquire, with creative financing, a range of equipment to support a new research lab. It may utilize an information-heavy, highly analytic approach performed by one or two key faculty or administrators, in a relatively informal process. On the other hand, a university performing a strategic assessment of its market potential may constitute a formal, participatory planning process which is richly supported by quantitative and qualitative information on the external environment.

Remember that many planning engagements can fail because of lack of adequate staff support. Information and analytic support can require significant staff resources—even for a process in which the information requirements are kept under control—and can become a tremendous resource sink for processes in which the information requested buries the participants in a blizzard of numbers and paper. In addition, managing and scheduling a planning process and structure can consume significant staff time. Often, a planning committee or planning process is constituted with inadequate thought being given to these matters. Don't fall into this trap.

Tactics for Implementation

A critical component of institutional planning is an awareness of the importance of implementation. One must set in motion planning activities and behaviors that will produce usable results quickly and in a manner likely to win support for the planning process. Even planning activities that are fundamentally long term and will not fully address the major problems at hand for some time should be devised to produce usable and useful results quickly. A number of examples reinforce this point:

- *Problem-focused planning that addresses particular institutional problems.* Even planning that is long range and/or strategic in nature could be used to address current problems. Such solutions build the credibility of the process.
- *External environmental scanning that yields important information about the institution's external environment.* This sort of product is useful to the institution even before the planning process is completed. In addition to being useful, it shows how planning is different from normal managerial activity that is internally and historically focused. Presidents and key faculty often have perspectives and contacts that enable them to make a major contribution to environmental scanning.
- *Useful collections and syntheses of information in a form not available from large-scale data bases.* It is critical that planning be supported by useful collections of information and combinations of information, with the emphasis on information that is distilled down to a useful level, not hopelessly expanded.
- *A planning process in which there is a bringing together of different parties is in itself beneficial.* In many cases, the process of planning can be more important than the plan or any of the planning products. The process can be a means of dealing with other issues and of resolving misunderstandings. It is a process of organizational learning.
- *A planning process that produces a clearly stated vision of the future that actually describes ways in which the organization will be changed*

and what the college or university or academic unit will be like in five years.

Remember: New or rejuvenated planning processes have a honeymoon period during which one needs to launch activities with a good grounding in planning concepts and insightful organizational analysis; produce some immediate dividends that will win and/or sustain supporters and weaken detractors; and chart one's planning on a course that will provide intermediate-term and long-term dividends to the organization. Time is limited, and one must use it wisely. The planner must also recognize that he must actively but subtly build support for planning—otherwise support may erode long before the planning cycle is complete.

An important aspect of a strategy for planning is to understand where the planning process is headed and what the product will be—and will not be. On the information front, the planning strategy should early on consider the combinations and distillations of information that will be reflected in the final plan or used as a basis for action. The nature of the decisions that will be supported should be understood. Your conception of the outcome of planning will probably change dramatically as the process proceeds.

A thought on the nature of plans: While there is a need for lengthy, detailed organizational plans for some purposes, most strategic plans should be short, highly focused, and lucid. Plans must communicate and even persuade. Your schedule should provide time and resources for generating executive summaries of organizational plans and five-page strategic plans that will be widely read and exercise influence.

Besides winning support for planning by creating usable products early on, tactics for implementation should continually strive to disarm critics and cultivate supporters in a variety of ways. It is a truism that planning cannot succeed without the blessing of the chief executive officer, and that blessing must be extended to include vice presidents and other key actors. The planner must continually manage the process to win new supporters and sustain those supporters already in the planning camp.

Planners must unashamedly plan for their own survival. Support for planning often ebbs and flows in organizations, and planners can survive best if they have other "lilypads" on which they can perch when planning is dormant or have other organizational and operational functions which they can perform when planning is not in vogue. Many planners have utilized such quiet times effectively as opportunities to develop analytic capabilities, to identify and prepare for new external challenges, and to tool up in preparation for the next round of active interest in planning. View these inevitable slow periods as opportunities and use them wisely.

Consolidated Organizational Analysis

In summary, the analysis of planning and launching of new planning activities should cover the topics summarized in Exhibit 8:

- What is the history of planning in your setting?
- Describe current planning activities
- Assess the opportunities and threats facing the organization
- What improvements/enhancements are needed in the planning activities?

Not every one of these topics and questions is equally important in every organizational setting, and some can be ignored. There is no best format for arraying the results of your organizational analysis; they should be in a form that makes sense to you and that can be communicated by you to others, such as your president, whom you may need to persuade. The important point is to think these topics through carefully and to structure the results so that you can comprehend the interrelationships among the characteristics of your planning environment. Moreover, you need to revisit your analysis over time as conditions and your level of insight change.

Conclusions on Your Chances for Success

To the new planner enticed into a planning venture by the honeyed words of a persuasive president or by the challenge of addressing serious issues facing the organization, much of our message may seem discouraging. Planning is serious business, challenged at every turn by existing power groups, unabashed detractors, and difficult, intractable issues; requiring theoretical understanding, the integration of theory and practice, insightful organizational analysis, and political acumen; and depending for success on hard work, the support of the president, and no small measure of luck.

The good news is that you don't need to be perfect or superhuman to be a successful planner. Most successful planners have at one time or another made most of the mistakes which we have described, but they have learned from their errors. What is deadly is to misunderstand profoundly the basic nature of planning and of your organization's challenges and to trap yourself in an inflexible planning structure that does not enable adaptation. If you understand how to play the planning game, you can be successful and

Exhibit 8:
Checklist for Analyzing Planning Environment and For Launching or Modifying Planning Activities

I. **History of planning in your setting**
- *Chronology of major planning activities*
- *Characteristics of major planning activities*
  - Style and content
  - Planning process/planning structure/analytic support
  - Major issues addressed
  - Successes/failures
  - Supporters/detractors

II. **Description of current planning activities**
- *What are the charges or management directives under which the different types of planning are occurring (strategic, long range, tactical, operational)?*
  - Issues that planning is directed to address
  - Content (elements, organizational units, resources)
  - Role of different planning participants (planning committees, planning support staff, line officers)
    - Identify critical issues
    - Assist others in performing studies
    - Coordinate assessments
    - Develop and examine alternatives
    - Advocate action
- *What are the characteristics of the different types of planning activities that are actually occurring? (strategic, tactical, operational)*
  - Structure
    - Selection   - Permanence
    - Composition   - Responsibility
  - Planning process
  - Analytic support
- *What are the mechanisms for linking the processes and results of the different types of planning?*
  - Strategic planning to organizational planning
  - Long term to tactical planning
  - Different types of tactical planning (e.g., program evaluation to resource allocation)
  - Tactical to operational planning
  - Overall organization of planning
    - Role of chief executive officer
    - Role of planning officer and staff
    - Linkage of planning to governance
    - Administrative responsibility for different types of planning
    - Communication network
  - What provisions are there for evaluating planning?
- *What are special limitations to the potentials for planning in your organization?*

Continues next page

Exhibit 8:
Checklist for Analyzing Planning Environment and For Launching or Modifying Planning Activities (continued)

III. Assessment of challenges facing the organization

- *What are the ten major challenges facing your organization?*
- *How many of these are external and how many are internal?*
- *How has planning been charged to deal with these challenges?*
- *What are emerging challenges in the future? How can planning deal with these today?*
- *How can you modify your planning activities (structure, process, analytic support) to confront these challenges?*

IV. Improvements in planning activities

- *What planning activities can be undertaken to yield immediate returns to build support for planning?*
- *What activities can be undertaken to improve and fine tune current planning cctivities?*
  - Strategic planning
  - Tactical planning
  - Operational planning
  - Improve linkages between different types of planning
  - Strengthen supports of planning
  - Overcome detractions of planning
  - Improve effectiveness of communication of results of planning

---

your organization can reap the benefits of healthy planning activities.

One should recognize that planning is not a cure for basic institutional ills. For example, excellent planning cannot overcome a fundamental lack of confidence between the president and faculty or a basic and widely held difference among key players over the institution's central mission and basic character. But planning can identify the problem and focus on the need for resolution.

3

Keep Moving Forward and Looking Back

As your planning process moves forward and begins to be judged on its performance and not on its promise, you will find that the unpleasant residue which you must get rid of will not be that of your predecessor—but your own! Do not be overly concerned; all planning activities produce some negative outcomes, pick up detractors along the way—in addition to those with which they began—and arouse opposition. Your challenge is to be certain that there are also sufficient positive elements to counterbalance the negative and to convince your leadership that planning is helping them to deal with problems which would have festered and emerged at a later point in a more onerous form. If you don't convince your leadership, then you may suffer the same fate, figuratively speaking, as the late messenger of bad tidings.

By moving forward and looking back, you can assess where you went awry and take corrective action. Planning processes, structures, and analytic support must be tuned and changed to adjust for clearer vision and for new challenges. No planning activity ever truly ends—what is past is prologue. The challenge is to focus your planning activities on emerging issues, challenges, and opportunities. Learning from past planning activities and facing new challenges is the hallmark of successful planning. In a sense this is what Cohen and March refer to as "planning in the future perfect tense:" using your experience with the past to confront new challenges and to posit what the future must be to deal with them. Planning-oriented behavior is not without its problems, but once you have tasted the challenge of helping your institution confront tomorrow's challenges today, you will not be content with your old challenges. Good luck—and good planning!

4

Conceptual Frameworks, Analytic Tools, and Worksheets to Help the Planner

Every planning process should be tailored to fit the needs of the particular setting. The starting and ending points are all different. No approach can be applied off the shelf. Few planning processes in higher education fit the classic models of comprehensive strategic planning processes. Nevertheless, some planners find it helpful to be guided by a comprehensive, conceptual framework of a planning process and by proven analytic tools that can be adapted to their setting. At the very least, it is valuable to take such frameworks and tools as points of reference.

Many of the newer planning textbooks have sound, usable analytic tools that the new planner can apply in planning for planning. They are less rigid and "prescriptive" than some of the early planning models. For example, John Bryson's *Strategic Planning for Public and Nonprofit Organizations* presents an excellent overall framework for a comprehensive, iterative, strategic-planning process and provides sample worksheets for particular products resulting from the planning process.

Exhibit 9 portrays an adaptation of Bryson's approach. Interested readers should consult Bryson's book, and tailor parts of his worksheets to the needs of their organization. Let us repeat the caveat: This exhibit suggests a more comprehensive and closely linked set of planning processes than is feasible in practice. It is a useful conceptual framework, but not a guide for designing a practical planning process in most collegiate settings.

The first activity in the process summarized in Exhibit 9 is to "Plan for Planning," which is the basic theme of this book. Just as "a problem well defined is a problem half solved," then "a planning process well planned is a planning process halfway to success." Much of this book has been devoted to becoming a successful student of the planning process.

The second set of activities is to assess the mission of the institution and/or academic unit and to assess stakeholder values regarding that mission. The increased complexity of academia's stakeholders makes this step especially important for today's and tomorrow's institution.

The third set of activities is to perform internal and external assessments that result in an analysis of strengths, weaknesses, opportunities, and threats (SWOT). This is a complex analysis which involves matching external possibilities with internal capabilities.

The fourth level involves developing and assessing strategic issues and actions that may be taken, these activities involve identifying strategic options and sketching their potential impact on stakeholders. This level leads to the development of strategies for the organization. These strategies should then be expressed in terms of a vision for the organization of the future, which describes how the organization will be affected by its new strategies.

Finally, these steps stimulate the tactical planning and implementation phases, which produce results that serve as feedback to future planning and visionary processes. This conceptual framework—and the set of analytic tools used at different stages—represents the current state of thinking about a planning process that meets the needs of an organization in a changing environment.

Experience in colleges and universities suggests that these steps tend to occur simultaneously rather than in sequence, as inferred from their logical presentation. The planner must help to link and coordinate these steps.

Exhibit 9:
A Conceptual Framework and Analytic Tools for Planning

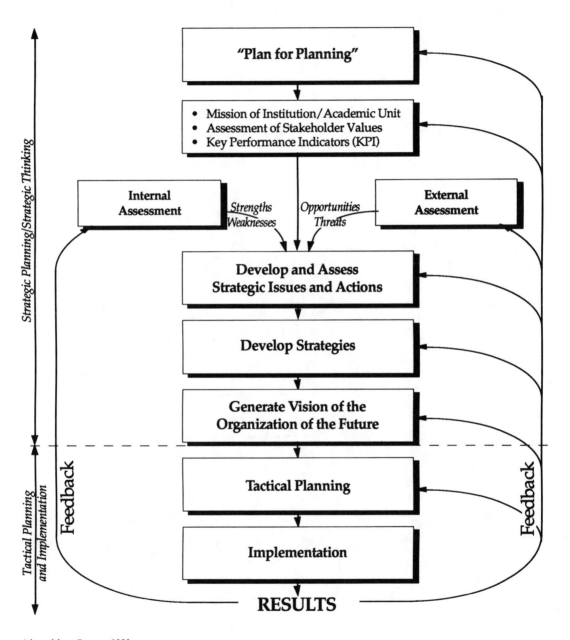

Adapted from Bryson, 1988

5

A Road Map of the Literature of Planning

As discussed, the new planner must use the literature on planning to sharpen insights on the principles of planning and to develop an ability to analyze the needs of the organization, the limitations of the role of planning, and the institutional history. Then the planner must develop and launch a strategy for planning within the context of sound planning principles.

A truly comprehensive bibliography of the literature of planning would consist of thousands of citations. Since planning is a pervasive behavior that is involved in every level of the strategic, management, and operational activities of organizations, there is scarcely an aspect of administrative behavior that is not somehow related to planning. But much of the planning literature is redundant, prescriptive and/or related to particular circumstances, or overly general in nature. The references contained in this monograph consist of many of the major, recent works on planning, divided into a number of categories relating to the level and functional areas of planning. As in all such bibliographies and classification schemes, many excellent works have been excluded, and those that have been included have been categorized broadly.

As you analyze and map the planning needs of your organization and devise a strategy for dealing with them, you should identify those aspects of planning on which information from the literature would assist your critical thinking. The following discussion begins with a brief historical context for evaluating and classifying the importance of different planning practices and their associated support literature. We then present a short list of basic references which we believe that all planners should have at their disposal regardless of the more specific planning issues of immediate concern in any particular setting. This list is followed by a selection of the most important references in several topical categories, with these references further subdivided into "critical," "recent," and "classic" selections, thus enabling a planner confronted with a particular set of challenges to assemble a reading list of ten or fifteen useful references for review. Remember, however, that the purpose of these readings is to assist you in critically analyzing your unique planning needs, not to find a cookbook answer in the literature.

The Evolution of Planning in Higher Education

This monograph would be very different if it had been written five, ten, or twenty years ago. The challenges and conditions facing higher education have changed significantly over that period, requiring changes in the nature of institutional decision making and in the techniques and applications of planning utilized by colleges and universities to support those decisions. Exhibits 10 and 11 summarize these developments by examining the characteristics of different eras of planning and decision making in higher education.

While the boundaries of the eras are somewhat artificial, they do suggest some interesting relationships. As the exhibits suggest, the late 1950s and early 1960s witnessed the growth of pressures for departure from the incremental, less participatory styles of planning and decision making that characterized the educational leadership of that period. Colleges and universities needed new approaches in order to deal with the tidal wave of new students and the growth of research and graduate study. Master planning and information-based decision making grappled with the facility needs and programmatic challenges posed not only by larger numbers of new students, but also by new student clienteles. The growing size and complexity of institutions were accompanied by more participatory decision making and some decentralization of power, although decision making continued to be largely incremental and political.

The attempt to apply management science techniques to higher education, a primary characteristic of the 1960s, denotes the decision making and planning style of this era as the *Age of Developing Quantitative Techniques*. The growth of administrative computing on campus began to make new information available to decision makers, and many experimented with quantitative models and other management science techniques at more progressive institutions. Examples of these quantitative techniques included Judy and Levine's Comprehensive Analytical Method for Planning in University Systems (CAMPUS) Model at the University of Toronto; the program of quantitative analysis and cost simulation research undertaken with Ford Foundation support at Berkeley; the Resource Requirements Prediction Model (RPPM) developed by the National Center for Higher Education Management Systems in the late 1960s/early 1970s; some quantitatively oriented approaches that were included in the Carnegie Commission's omnibus series of

Exhibit 10:
Eras in Planning and Decision Making

Era	Conditions	Primary Focus	Nature of Institutional Decision Making	Nature of Planning and Strategy Formulation
1950s AGE OF AUTHORITY	• Relatively stable conditions • Goal consensus • New institutional types • Steady growth	• Facilities • New institution studies	• Less participatory, administrative fiat	• Continuation of traditional, less sophisticated modes of planning and strategy
1960s AGE OF DEVELOPING QUANTITATIVE TECHNIQUES	• Rapid growth in enrollment masks many problems • Expansion embraces new student clienteles • Student dissension changes relationships	• Facilities • Institution self-studies • New programs • Student studies	• More participatory • Dispersal of power • Talk rational, but decision making continues to be predominantly incremental, political, non-rationalistic	• Physical master planning • Experimentation with management science techniques • Emergence of institutional research and planning • State system planning
1970s AGE OF PRAGMATIC APPLICATION	• Stabilizing enrollments • Revenue shortfalls • Need to reallocate resources to deal with imbalances caused by 1960s growth • Selective growth and retrenchment and promise of decline in 1980s • Goal fragmentation	• Internal orientation • Existing programs • Resources • Efficiency • Recruitment • State relations	• Reallocation mentality • Incremental, imperfect decision making continues • Some institutions take advantage of continued growth in late 1970s to prepare for 1980s • Others wait for conditions to get so bad they will have to act	• Comprehensive master plans • Program planning and evaluation • Resource reallocation • Management of decline • New techniques and advances in management science applications • Planning as staff function • Strategic management emerges in late 1970s
1980s AGE OF STRATEGIC REDIRECTION	• Substantial decline in numbers of traditional college cohorts, but increase in collegiate enrollments • Decline in some institutions, substantial regional and institutional variations • Resource shortfalls • Changes in student characteristics • Need to invest large sums in computing, scientific equipment, and capital plant for research and graduate education	• External orientation • Effectiveness • Quality • Outcomes • Competitive advantage • Economic development • Telematics	• Proactive relationship to environment • External environment affects internal decision making • Continued imperfections in decision making, but harsh penalties for poor decisions or deferral of choices • Enhanced use of analysis and decision support systems • Information management is key	• Strategic planning gains popularity • Re-emergence of master planning • Selective focus on new clienteles, new partnerships, external relationships • Experiences with shortcomings of analysis and planning • Emphasis on applications rather than techniques • Planning as line function, dispersed through organization

From NORRIS & POULTON in PETERSON & METS (1987)

Exhibit 10:
Eras in Planning and Decision Making (continued)

Era	Conditions	Primary Focus	Nature of Institutional Decision Making	Nature of Planning and Strategy Formulation
1990s **AGE OF RETRENCHMENT AND REALLOCATION**	• Varying demography • Economic recession in early 1990s • Resource shortfalls • Changing student characteristics • Need to invest large sums in computing, scientific equipment, buildings • Global, international challenges • Opportunities for new partnerships/relationships	• Internal reallocation • External focus to make up for resource inadequacies • Competitive	• Reactive, somewhat proactive • Focus on cost cutting and productivity enhancement • Use tools of retrenchment and reallocation • Questioning of institutional costs and patterns of delivery • Combination of internal and external decision making	• Focus on approaches to cost containment, quality, and productivity enhancement • Cross-disciplinary teams • Emphasis on insight and applications • Planning as line function • Strategic and tactical planning are mainstream
AND/OR				
1990s **AGE OF NEW PARADIGMS FOR UNIVERSITIES**	• Varying demography • Economic recession in early 1990s • Resource shortfalls • Changing student characteristics • Need to invest large sums in computing, scientific equipment, buildings • Global, international challenges • Opportunities for new partnerships/relationships	• External focus on new roles and resources • Internal focus to change administrative and academic cultures • Competitive • Science/industry and economic development • Technology	• Proactive • Focus on key strategies • Use tools of retrenchment and of transformation • Questioning of patterns of delivery • Use of decision support/information management • Achieve better operational integration • Develop a service-oriented approach to program delivery • Bold new alliances and initiatives	• Develop transformational approaches to academic and administrative culture • Empower academic and administrative units farther down the organization • Cross-disciplinary teams, consultation, not consensus • Focus on new clienteles, new partnerships, external relationships • Emphasis on insight and applications • New skill sets required: a service orientation for global, distributed universities • Planning as a line function • Transformational, strategic management is mainstream

From NORRIS & POULTON in PETERSON & METS (1987)

studies on higher education; and the development of enrollment projection and manpower forecasting techniques. During this period, institutional research and quantitative support of planning grew in institutions. Rourke and Brooks captured the changing nature of institutional decision making in *The Managerial Revolution in Higher Education*, which described the growing influence of information, research, and objective criteria in decision making. But the planning, strategy, and policy challenges facing institutions in the 1960s dealt with choosing among positive alternatives, namely providing greater resources devoted to expanding higher education. More difficult challenges would follow in the 1970s.

The development of management science support tools continued at an increased pace into the 1970s as more mature versions of tools introduced in the 1960s were used to help shape plans, strategies, and policies. Initially, the emphasis continued to be more on technique, rather than on application. But the overriding strategic-planning issue in the 1970s was selective growth and retrenchment, rather than overall expansion. Through the research and analytical approaches of David Breneman, Allan Cartter, Richard Freeman, and others, colleges and universities identified the possibilities of enrollment declines driven by demographic changes, surpluses of doctoral-educated professionals, and other manpower imbalances. By the last half of the 1970s, authors began to speak of education in terms of the "management of decline." Resource allocation and redistribution challenges spawned the use of new sets of qualitative and quantitative analytical approaches that dealt with difficult choices and trade-offs among competing resource demands. Quantitative financial-planning models, such as EDUCOM's Educational Financial Planning Model, supported this thrust. Institutional research and planning grew in support of these functions, and planners increasingly served as staff in developing formal, often comprehensive, planning processes in many colleges and universities. Much of the thrust of planning was reactive, however, responding to environmental conditions after they became clear. The focus on problem solving and planning under apparently immutable conditions of fiscal stress led us to characterize the 1970s era as the *Age of Pragmatism*.

Another significant legacy of the 1970s was a healthy awareness on the part of decision makers of the limitations of different planning and policy support tools. The professional literature on management science, operations research, management information systems, and planning had offered decision makers tools that were overly prescriptive and technical, often inflexible, and unduly focused on techniques, to the exclusion of many critical factors of

Exhibit 11:
Development of Institutional Planning Activities

Dimension	1950s	1960s	1970s	1980s	1990s
ACADEMIC	• Institutional self-study • New units	• Student studies • New institutions	• Program planning, evaluation • Enrollment forecasting • Recruitment need/demand	• Marketing • Retention • Human resources • Outcomes • Replacement • New Priorities • New delivery systems • New roles/behaviors	• Fundamental assessment of academic delivery systems • Diverse populations • Continuing learning • Marketing/retention • New delivery systems • Technology changing faculty roles/student roles • Infusion of technology
PHYSICAL	• Campus • Facility	• Space utilization	• Facility condition • Energy • Retro-fitting	• Replacement • Learning network of campus/environs	• Renovation/retrofit • New science and technology facilities • Distributed facilities • "University district"
RESOURCES	• Early fiscal analysis	• Budget projections	• PPBS and other budget strategies • Modeling, simulation • Financial forecasting • Cost-benefit	• Planning software • Capital financing • Fund raising • Information as resource • New sources	• Examination of costs and productivity • Fund raising • Resource allocation/retrenchment • Focus on centers of excellence
OTHER			• Master planning • State relations	• Environmental scanning • Futuring • Regional or economic development • New partnership	• Partnerships between higher education and industry • Education for a global economy • Distributed learning and research

Adapted from PETERSON (1986)

successful implementation. Program budgeting, zero-based budgeting, and related techniques of resource allocation and budgetary support ignored many of the realities of the functioning organization. The title of Aaron Wildavsky's article, "If Planning is Everything, Maybe It's Nothing," suggests the frustration with oversold techniques and formalized, prescriptive approaches.

By the start of the 1980s, decision makers had begun to embrace "strategic management" as a way of managing an organization with an eye to the environment. The conditions of potential demographic decline carried over into the 1980s, but colleges and universities were confronted with additional challenges that required more enlightened action than merely dividing up pieces of a smaller and smaller pie. Changing student characteristics—such as increases in older students, international students, and Hispanic and Oriental minority students—required more proactive responses. There were also needs to invest huge sums of money in new information and telecommunications systems, personal computers, scientific equipment, and capital plant for research and graduate education. Opportunities and challenges arose for universities to join with industry and government in support of economic development. Faculty shortfalls in growth areas such as business and engineering had to be overcome. These and similar issues turned the attention of leadership to a focus on external developments and alternate funding resources outside the university.

These challenges encouraged leaders to move beyond incremental solutions and focus on strategic planning approaches which also have emerged during this period. Keller characterizes these approaches as a "third way" that incorporates the best aspects of rational and political/incremental decision making. More leaders are taking proactive stances in examining the environment rather than the reactive stances that have traditionally characterized responses to decline. Master planning has re-emerged but with a more proactive, change-agent orientation and with a greater focus on outcomes, program quality, and institutional effectiveness.

During the 1980s, these changes altered the focus of both the current and future activities of planning, strategy, and policy formulation for institutional decision makers. Information and analysis continued to be critical, but less importance was placed upon technique, and more emphasis was given to distilling information to a manageable level and limiting its use in a manner appropriate for the given application. Planning support remained a staff function, but planning itself came to be seen as a line function, the responsibility of institutional leaders. The institution/environment interface was seen as more complex. The institution was seen as more able to adapt to environmental challenges than was previously the case. Institutional leaders found themselves in an *Age of Strategic Redirection*, with planning, strategy, and policy focusing on quality, outcomes, and external relationships.

As planners in higher education confront the challenges of the 1990s, they can avail themselves of strategic planning skills and orientations that will serve them well. However, the challenges and opportunities of the 1990s are perplexing. On one hand, the economic impact of recession in the early years of the 1990s, demands that the cost of higher education be controlled, and pressure for productivity improvement will cause a wave of retrenchment and cutbacks, much like the "management of decline" efforts of the late 1970s.

On the other hand, the opportunities facing higher education to use technology to achieve distributed learning and research networks, to enhance the curriculum, and to address the educational needs of hypergrowth metropolitan areas are as exciting as any that have ever faced our nation's postsecondary education enterprises. The need to "internationalize" education to prepare students for a global economy and society is broadly recognized. Efforts to revive and revitalize undergraduate instruction hold much promise and a strong imperative. The need to achieve diversity and inclusiveness in educational organizations is receiving even greater attention.

To meet these challenges, universities are seeking new paradigms of operation that will enable them to address their traditional roles with greater effectiveness and to reach out to new partnerships to address serious opportunities and obligations.

So the 1990s are a potential mixed metaphor: an *Age of Retrenchment and Reallocation* existing side by side with an *Age of New Educational Paradigms*. Standing on the front-edge of the 1990s, it is difficult to say which metaphor will prevail. The financial exigencies of the early 1990s and institutional resistance to fundamental change are sufficiently great that the early 1990s are likely to be characterized by retrenchment and reallocation. By the late 1990s, there is a reasonable hope that institutions will have developed the capacity to generate new approaches for taking advantage of the exciting opportunities.

How Literature and Research Have Kept Pace with the Field

Higher education has always drawn heavily from other disciplines to support its planning endeavors. Many of the seminal articles and books on management applications in higher education were developed as specialized applications by economists, social psychologists, or political scientists examining higher education as an interesting and underdeveloped field of study. The following "classics" remain useful as a basic foundation of applications and illustrate how this area has drawn from other fields.

From business and corporate planning, higher education has drawn from many basic texts that have stimulated thought on planning and strategy formulation. Examples include Herbert Simon's *Administrative Behavior*; Robert Anthony's *Planning and Control Systems*; Robert Ackoff's *A Concept of Corporate Planning* and *Creating the Corporate Future*; Peter Drucker's works, including *Management: Tasks, Responsibilities and Practices*; David Ewing's *The Human Side of Planning*; Schendel and Hofer's *Strategic Management: A New View of Business Policy*; and DeGues' *Planning as Learning*.

Political science and public administration have yielded the best works on policy analysis, especially in the public sector, on the importance of implementation, and on the politics of the budget process. Charles Lindblom's articles on "The Science of Muddling Through" and "Still Muddling, Not Yet Through" cast light on the strengths and limitations of incrementalism. Rourke and Brooks' *The Managerial Revolution in Higher Education* was a political science venture into higher education. Bardach's *The Implementation Game* contains many lessons for higher education, as does Wildavsky's *The Politics of the Budgetary Process*.

From organizational behavior have come contributions that have focused on the higher education setting, such as Burton Clark's "The Organizational Saga in Higher Education," Cohen and March's *Leadership and Ambiguity*, and March's "Emerging Developments in the Study of Organizations." Havelock's *Change Agent's Guide to Innovation in Education* and Rogers and Shoemaker's *Communication of Innovations* applied the concepts of the diffusion of innovations to a variety of organizational settings, including higher education. Benveniste's *The Politics of Expertise* and *Mastering the Politics of Planning* are major works that are helpful to understanding planning in higher education.

Management science has applied many techniques developed in other settings to higher education. Most have focused on operational, rather than strategic, issues. Several books which have dealt with management science applications in higher education have included Balderston's *Managing Today's University*, Hopkins and Massey's *Planning Models for Colleges and Universities*, Lawrence and Service's *Quantitative Approaches to Higher Education Management*, and Anthony and Herzlinger's *Management Control in Non-Profit Organizations*.

Over the past decade, literature on the management of nonprofit organizations has been taken more seriously by university leaders as a source of insight, some of which is highly applicable to colleges and universities. John Bryson's *Strategic Planning for Public and Nonprofit Organizations* is widely accepted as a near classic in the field. Peter Drucker has drawn attention to the excellence of management and strategic thinking in the nonprofit sector, and many educational leaders could learn from the strategic visioning practiced by many associations and other nonprofit organizations.

As technology has become more important to higher education, the literature on information technology and telecommunications applications in colleges and universities has become popular not just with technologists, but with presidents, vice presidents, and the new breed of technology administrators, the "chief information officer." Influential works have included Hawkins' *Organizing and Managing Information Resources on Campus*; Heterick's *Ivory Towers, Silicon Basements*; Gilbert and Green's *Making Computers Work for Administrators*; John McCredie's *Campus Computing Strategies*; and Kenneth Wood's *Campus Networking Strategies*. Information technology will reshape our campuses—and extend their reach—even more profoundly in the 1990s.

Other techniques (both genuinely new wine and old wine in new bottles) from other organizational sectors are continuing to impact planning and management in higher education. Total Quality Management (TQM) is a major issue in enhancing quality in design and manufacture and is being utilized to fundamentally change attitudes and practices in those areas. Authors like Chaffee and Sher are applying the precepts of TQM to higher education with intriguing results and promise. Moreover, the lessons learned from the reconfiguration of business organizations in the 1980s are being applied to other sectors, including education. Much of the thinking behind the new paradigms for academic and administrative culture derive from this work. During the 1990s, this will be an important topic.

The relationships among the literature, research, and practice of planning in higher education follow a pattern typical of the diffusion and adoption of innovations. Fundamental organizational research or new techniques originate in the social science disciplines or the applied management disciplines, as noted. Problems and pressing issues in higher education prompt inquiry and research on the application of the emerging concepts or techniques to the higher education setting. Leading institutions experiment with new ideas, such as Stanford University's application of financial-planning models, establishment of a computer-intensive environment, and most recently, seeking new paradigms for academic and administrative culture. Articles on pioneering applications gain attention. As results emerge and trends are identified, a major review is published highlighting the developments of an era. Rourke and Brooks' *Managerial Revolution in High Education* and Keller's *Academic Strategy* are two of several such examples. These volumes prompt dissemination and provide interest in further research into higher education applications. As the area matures further, the emphasis continues to shift to insightful application and becomes part of the accepted practice of higher education.

With the development of a larger cadre of higher education professionals who have greater sophistication in planning techniques and applications, there will continue to be increased interest in developing and researching these applications. However, it is likely that new concepts will continue to come from the basic social science and management science disciplines, and the cutting edge will continue to reside with educational leaders who experiment with applying new techniques in leading institutions. The true critical success factor in planning is insightful application, not technical virtuosity, and by the time an approach reaches that state of evolution, it is part of the mainstream of planning.

A concluding word is in order on the state of research on planning in higher education. Recent research on planning has focused on planning as an organizational strategy and approach (Schmidtlein and Milton). Earlier work by Michael in *Learning to Plan/Planning to Learn* focused on the social psychology of planning and on how planning organizations behave differently. But what is lacking is extensive research on planners—who they are, what makes them different, and how this contributes to making "planning-oriented behavior" different from "management-oriented behavior." Even without a formal planning process, the planning orientation of individuals seems to be what differentiates people and results in planning-oriented behavior. Hopefully, research in the 1990s could sketch in some of the gaps in our knowledge on this subject.

A Short List of References

The particular collection of readings which the planner needs to review depends upon the nature of the challenges which he is facing and his background. In our judgment, there is a short list of references that are especially good in discussing the historical context of planning and decision making in higher education, the concepts of strategic planning and futures techniques, and a wide variety of strategic and tactical planning topics. Exhibit 12 describes in a summary fashion the contents and typical areas covered by our recommended short list. The following section provides annotations for each entry of the short list.

In reality, the planner should choose from this short list and from the more detailed bibliography that follows, a more extensive, tailored selection of readings that fit the needs of the situation. The bibliographic listing is organized by topic area, with each topic area further subdivided into "critical" reading, "recent" selections, and "classic" selections.

Bryson, J. M. *Strategic Planning for Public and Nonprofit Organizations*. San Francisco: Jossey-Bass, 1988.

In this book, John M. Bryson explains a variety of approaches to help leaders and managers of public and nonprofit organizations fulfill their missions and satisfy their constituents through strategic planning. Bryson incorporates the best private sector methods into a new strategic-planning process for the public and nonprofit sector. He provides examples of successful and unsuccessful efforts at strategic planning, offers practical advice on how to overcome obstacles, and shows how to implement a planning process that has been used successfully by a number of public and nonprofit organizations. The book is not specifically designed for higher education, but is clearly applicable. It also includes such valuable resources as sample strategic-planning worksheets, methods for managing a strategic issue, and more.

Mintzberg, H. "Crafting Strategy." *Harvard Business Review*, 1987, 66-77.

This is an excellent, highly readable article that captures Henry Mintzberg's supple understanding of how strategy is really crafted in organizations. His broad experience in corporations, universities, and other organizations is clear. His ideas regarding emergent strategies are splendid for the college and university planner.

Schendel, D. E., and Hofer, C. W., eds. *Strategic Management: A New View of Business Policy and Planning*. Boston: Little, Brown, 1979.

This volume is based on a collection of papers commissioned for a 1977 conference. The objectives were these: 1) to define the dimensions and boundaries of business policy, strategic management, and planning; 2) to identify opportunities for reasearch; and

Exhibit 12:
A Critical Short List of Planning References

Source	Description	Topical Area
Bryson, J.M. *Strategic Planning for Public and Nonprofit Organizations* San Francisco: Jossey-Bass 1988	An excellent, comprehensive text for planning for nonprofit organizations – easily adapted to colleges and universities.	Strategic Planning
Mintzberg, H. "Crafting Strategy" *Harvard Business Review* 1987	An insightful article on how strategy is fashioned and utilized in organizations.	Strategic Planning
Schendel and Hofer *Strategic Management: A New View of Business Policy and Planning* 1979	Blend of theory, research, and practice of strategic management in business and higher education.	Strategic Planning/ Strategic Management
Keller, G. *Academic Strategy: The Management Revolution in American Higher Education* 1983	Historical development of planning and emergence of strategic planning. Excellent insights.	Strategic Planning/ History of Planning/ Critique of Planning/ University Application
Shirley, R. "Identifying the Levels of Strategy for a College or University," *Long Range Planning* 1983	Alternate framework for linking strategy and management in higher education.	Strategic Planning/ Strategic Management/ University Application
Cope, R. *Opportunity from Strength: Strategic Planning Clarified with Case Studies* Washington, D.C.: ASHE-ERIC Higher Education Report, No. 8, 1987	Upgraded discussion of "contextual strategic planning" illustrated with eleven case studies.	Strategic Planning/ Case Studies
Steeples, D. "Successful Strategic Planning Case Studies," *New Directions for Higher Education,* No. 64 San Francisco: Jossey-Bass 1988	An interesting anthology of eight case studies, with analysis of strategic planning by Robert Shirley.	Strategic Planning/ Case Studies
Schmidtlein, F.A. and Milton, T.H. "Adapting Strategic Planning to Campus Realities" 1990	An excellent anthology of five case studies, with analysis by Frank Schmidtlein.	Strategic Planning/ Case Studies

Continued on next page

Exhibit 12:
A Critical Short List of Planning References (continued)

Source	Description	Topical Area
Birnbaum, R. *How Colleges Work: The Cybernetics of Academic Organization and Leadership.* San Francisco: Jossey-Bass, 1988	Examines four models of how universities work – collegial, bureaucratic, political, and organized anarchy.	Planning Context
Chaffee, E.E. and Tierney, W.G. *Collegiate Cultures and Leadership Strategies* New York: McMillan, 1988	An excellent book on the practices of leadership and planning in the collegiate context.	Planning Context
Cohen, M.D. and March, J.G. *Leadership and Ambiguity: The American College President* 1986	Explores the decision-making environment in which planning operates – introduces the "organized anarchy" model.	Planning Context
Massy, W.F. and Zemsky, R. *The Dynamics of Academic Productivity* Denver: SHEEO, 1990	An important work exploring the components of academic productivity.	Planning Context/ Enhancing Academic Productivity
"The Lattice and the Ratchet" *Policy Perspectives* The PEW Foundation 1990	Excellent description of administrative and academic pressures that have led to burgeoning costs.	Planning Context/ Enhancing Academic Productivity
Elmore, R.F. "Backward Mapping: Implementation Research and Policy Decisions" *Political Science Quarterly* 1980	An article yielding important insights on the difficulties of policy implementation and planning.	Planning Context/ Strategic Planning/ Tactical Planning
Peterson, M. and Mets, L. *Governance, Management and Leadership: An Annotated Guide To Key Resources* 1987	A comprehensive, up-to-date reference on not only planning, but also on governance, management and leadership in higher education. A must reference.	All Topical Areas
Morrison, J.L., Renfro, W.L., and Boucher, W.I. *Futures Research and the Strategic Planning Process: Implications for Higher Education* 1984	Discusses the details of futures techniques and the integration of futures techniques with strategic planning and details techniques.	Futures Technique/ Strategic Planning

3) to help researchers, practitioners, and students better understand the implications of these newer approaches to organizational integration. Ten topics are covered, including strategy and strategic management; goals and goal formation; strategy formulation, evaluation, and implementation; theory building and testing; and practitioners' views. Although oriented toward business, one chapter is concerned with not-for-profit organizations, including higher education. References to the higher education literature are dated. Nevertheless, this reference contains a blend of theory, research, and practice, and provides a useful source for those seeking to understand the historical roots of the strategic policy and planning area.

Shirley, R. C. "Identifying the Levels of Strategy for a College or University." *Long Range Planning,* 1983, *16* (3), 92-98.

Shirley outlines six decision areas that accomplish the overall function of strategy and discusses how they apply to the nonprofit sector, specifically higher education. The six areas include basic mission, clientele, goals, program/service mix, geographic service area, and comparative advantage. Shirley also contrasts four levels of decision making in the university. These levels include institutional strategy, campus-wide functional strategies, program strategies, and program-level functional strategies. This article is important for the planner and institutional leader, for it provides an operational, decision-based framework for organizing a strategic-planning process and shows how strategy at the institutional level gets translated into strategy plus tactical and operational plans at the program level.

Cope, R. *Opportunity From Strength: Strategic Planning Clarified with Case Studies.* Washington, D.C.: ASHE-ERIC Higher Education Reports, No. 8, 1987.

This book provides an updated version of Cope's notions on conceptual strategic planning. Cope's concepts are illustrated by eleven case studies demonstrating a wide variety of strategic-planning approaches.

Steeples, D., ed. New Directions for Higher Education. *Successful Strategic Planning: Case Studies, No. 64.* San Francisco: Jossey-Bass, 1988.

This case study anthology contains eight useful examples of planning in a wide variety of campus settings. In the first chapter, Robert Shirley provides an excellent overview of strategic planning.

Schmidtlein, F. A., and Milton, T. H., eds. "Adapting Strategic Planning to Campus Realities." *New Directions for Institutional Research* No. 64, Fall 1990.

This excellent volume showcases five case studies of strategic planning in very different settings. In each setting, the particular approach to strategic planning was adapted to the needs of the particular setting and to the challenges and opportunities confronting the institutions. A final chapter by Frank Schmidtlein interprets how these five strategic-planning efforts have related to institutional character, issues confronting the institutions, and the role of planning support.

Birnbaum, R. *How Colleges Work: Patterns of Organization, Management and Leadership in Higher Education*. San Francisco: Jossey-Bass, 1988.

This book applies contemporary organizational theory and psychology to the world of higher education and enables the reader to make sense of the complex patterns of organization in today's institutions of higher learning. No single approach will help solve all the complex administrative problems in higher education, so Birnbaum examines four models—to illuminate the key dimensions of every college and university. Next he explains why flexible systems of organization that take all four dimensions into account are essential in higher education. He then integrates the best features of these models into a flexible new model of college and university organization and shows how this model can help academic leaders more fully understand colleges and universities and enhance their own professional performance.

Chaffee, E. E., and Tierney, W. G. *Collegiate Culture and Leadership Strategies*. New York: MacMillan, 1988.

This book is a useful companion to Birnbaum's work. It focuses on the relationship between collegiate cultures and the practice of leadership. The authors describe three systems of strategy—linear, adaptive, and interpretive—that operate in a particular institutional setting. Each approach to strategy contributes to the institutions' effectiveness.

Cohen, M. D., and March, J. G. *Leadership and Ambiguity: The American College President*. 2nd edition. Harvard Business School Press, 1986.

Only half of this volume deals specifically with the careers, images, functions, and tenure of the college president. The other half describes models of governance and the process of choice in the university. The university is characterized as an "organized anarchy," i.e., an organization that had problematic goals, unclear technology, and fluid participation. The tasks of goal setting, planning, and organization change are among many topics discussed. The volume includes advice on how to facilitate action in the university setting; hence it is a valuable reference to the practitioner.

Keller, G. *Academic Strategy: The Management Revolution in American Higher Education*. Baltimore: Johns Hopkins University Press, 1983.

This book resulted from a nationwide study of management practices in a wide variety of colleges and universities in the early 1980s. Keller describes the historical development of planning, management leadership in higher education, and the emerging emphasis on academic strategy and strategic planning. He describes academic strategies as a means of moving beyond the limitations of normative, rigid planning, on the one hand, and traditional incrementalism, on the other. Keller provides excellent discussions of the contextual and historical development of planning in higher education, the strengths and limitations of incrementalism and perspective planning, and the importance of leadership. The bibliography and references are essential to any planner. His characterizations of success factors for planning are good, but are more abstract than operational. This publication played a fundamental role in the mid-1980s of shifting the attention of institutional planners to strategic planning. Many of the newer works on strategic planning in higher education and in other nonprofit settings have refined and applied strategic-planning techniques. However, Keller's book is still a classic and critical reference.

Elmore, R. F. "Backward Mapping: Implementation Research and Policy Decisions." *Political Science Quarterly*, 1979-80, 94 (4), 601-616.

Elmore contends that most policy making is flawed because it focuses on the front end of the policy-making process, which contends with goals, organizational intent, and hierarchy, rather than with the back end of the policy-making process, namely implementation, where 90 percent of the variation between policy intent and actuality occurs. Elmore suggests backward mapping: a process in which policy makers examine how and by whom policies will be implemented and then craft their policies to recognize the characteristics of the implementers and the variability and situational nature of the implementation environment. This is an excellent, context-establishing article which yields important insights on the difficulties of policy implementation. It has useful insights for planners, too, who must deal with the uncertainties of extrapolating the impacts of plans on operating units and understand how strategy and tactics are translated and filtered by implementing units.

Peterson, M. W., and Mets, L. A., eds. *Key Resources on Higher Education Governance, Management and Leadership.* San Francisco: Jossey-Bass, 1987.

This volume is a current, comprehensive guide to reference resources on governance, management, and leadership in higher education intended for use by practicing administrators, faculty, and students. Each chapter presents an overview of the topic, a framework for organizing the literature, and a commentary on how the literature has developed and on the current status of the topic. The annotations contain evaluative comments about how and to whom the work may be useful. A wide range of subtopics, encompassing all areas of strategic and tactical planning, are covered in more than twenty chapters. This is a critical volume for planners.

Morrison, J. L.; Renfro, W. L.; and Boucher, W. I. *Futures Research and the Strategic Planning Process: Implications for Higher Education.* ASHE-ERIC Higher Education Research Report No. 9. Washington, D.C.: Association for the Study of Higher Education, 1984.

This publication presents a concise, yet thorough, development of a strategic-planning process that combines the more traditional long-range planning cycle (goal setting, implementing, monitoring, and forecasting) with an environmental-scanning cycle (scanning, evaluation/ranking, forecasting, and monitoring). The former maintains an internal perspective, while the latter is directed externally. Six components are discussed, giving special attention to the techniques (including examples) of environmental scanning, issues evaluation, and forecasting. Discussions cover many topics ranging across scanning taxonomies, impact networks, the Delphi technique, cross-impact analysis, scenario building, and others. A valuable reference source for the leader, planner, or faculty member new to the applications of futures techniques, this publication also provides many citations for pursuing techniques and applications in greater depth. For the interested reader, other citations on futuring and related techniques are contained later in this bibliography.

6

Bibliography of Planning

In addition to the short list of references cited in the preceding chapter, there is a wealth of general and specialized readings on the subject of planning. Exhibit 13 summarizes the organizational framework which is used to present these readings.

Nature and History of Planning

A significant portion of the planning literature deals with basic definitions, theories, and principles of planning, and/or the history of planning in higher education. If not selected carefully, the general planning literature can be prescriptive, normative, and unsuited to the higher education environment. The works we have selected here provide both a sound definitional basis and a grounding in historical development that serve as a road map in applying planning in higher education.

Critical Reading

DeGeus, A. P. "Planning as Learning." *Harvard Business Review*, March/April 1988, 70–74.

Keller, G. *Academic Strategy: The Management Revolution in American Higher Education*. Baltimore: Johns Hopkins University Press, 1983.

Peterson, M. W. "Analyzing Alternative Approaches to Planning." In P. Jedamus, M. W. Peterson, and Associates, *Improving Academic Management*. San Francisco: Jossey-Bass, 1980, 113–163.

Schmidtlein, Frank A., and Milton, Toby H. "College and University Planning: Perspectives from a Nation-Wide Study." *Planning for Higher Education*, 1988, 17 (3), 1–20.

Exhibit 13:
Topic Areas in the Planning Bibliography

TRADITIONAL CATEGORIES	AREAS OF GROWING FUTURE IMPORTANCE
Nature and History of Planning	**Futuring, Issues Management, and Environmental Scanning**
Planning Context	**Competitive Advantage**
Critique of Planning	**Partnerships among Education, Industry, and Government**
Strategic Planning/ Strategic Management	**Institutional Effectiveness, Outcomes, and Quality**
Tactical Planning • Budgeting and Resource Allocation • Retrenchment and Management of Decline • Program Evaluation/Techniques of Evaluation • Academic Planning • Enrollment Planning and Management • Campus and Facilities Planning	**Information Technology and Telecommunications**
	Faculty/Administrative Manpower and Workplace Issues
	Changes in America and the University of the 21st Century
Decision Support for Planning	**Global/International Education**
	Public Sector and Nonprofit Management

Recent Selections

Hickson, D. J.; Butler, R. J.; Cray, D.; Mallory, G. R.; and Wilson, D. C. *Top Decisions: Strategic Decision-Making in Organizations.* Oxford, England: Basil Blackwell, 1986.

Jauch, L. R., and Kraft, K. L. "Strategic Management of Uncertainty." *Academy of Management Review*, 1986, *11* (4), 77–79.

Jenster, P. "Using Critical Success Factors in Planning." *Long-Range Planning*, 1987, *20* (4).

Hudson, B. "Planning: Typologies, Issues, and Application Contexts." *Planning and Vocational Education.* Edited by G. H. Copa and J. Moss. New York: McGraw-Hill, 1983, 18–44.

McConkie, D. D. "Planning for Uncertainty." *Business Horizons*, 1987, 40–45.

Norris, D. M., and Mims, R. S. "A New Maturity for Institutional Planning and Information Management." *Journal of Higher Education*, 1984, *55* (6), 700–718.

Pennings, J. M., and Associates. *Organizational Strategy and Change.* San Francisco: Jossey-Bass, 1985.

Peterson, M. W. "Continuity, Challenge and Change: An Organizational Perspective on Planning Past and Future." *Planning for Higher Education*, 1986, *14* (3), 6–15.

Classic Selections

Ackoff, Russell L. *Creating the Corporate Future.* New York: John Wiley & Sons, 1981.

Anthony, R. N. *Planning and Control Systems: A Framework for Analysis.* Cambridge, MA: Harvard University Press, 1965.

Balderston, F. E. *Managing Today's University.* San Francisco: Jossey-Bass, 1974.

Bracker, J. "The Historical Development of the Strategic Management Concept." *Academy of Management Review*, 1980, *5* (2), 219–224.

Friedman, J., and Hudson, B. "Knowledge and Action: A Guide to Planning Theory." *Journal of the American Institute of Planners*, 1974, *40* (1), 2–16.

Jones, L. R. "A Historical Survey of Academic Planning Development." *Planning for Higher Education*, 1979, 7 (5), 21–27.

Michael, D. N. *On Learning to Plan and Planning to Learn*. San Francisco: Jossey-Bass, 1973.

Richardson, R. C.; Gardner, D. E.; and Pierce, A. "The Need for Institutional Planning." *ERIC Research Currents*, September 1977.

Rourke, F., and Brooks, G. *The Managerial Revolution in Higher Education*. Baltimore: Johns Hopkins University Press, 1966.

Sibley, W. H. "Planning for Universities: The Contemporary Predicament." *International Journal of Institutional Management in Higher Education*, 1977, *1* (2), 85–96.

Planning Context

The decision-making context in higher education must be understood if the planner is to apply successfully the concepts of planning. This understanding is critical in interpreting some of the planning texts which have excellent theoretical content but have been developed and written for the business environment. The following selections are especially helpful in establishing this planning context.

Critical Reading

Birnbaum, Robert. *How Colleges Work: Patterns of Organization, Management, and Leadership In Higher Education*. San Francisco: Jossey-Bass, 1988.

Chaffee, E. E., and Tierney, W. G. *Collegiate Cultures and Leadership Strategies*. New York: MacMillan, 1988.

Cohen, M. D., and March, J. G. *Leadership and Ambiguity: The American College President*. New York: McGraw-Hill, 1974.

Davis, Stanley M. *Future Perfect*. Reading, MA: Addison-Wesley, 1987.

Drucker, Peter F. *The New Realities*. New York: Harper and Row, 1989.

Elmore, R. F. "Backward Mapping: Implementation Research and Policy Decisions." *Political Science Quarterly*, 1979–80, *94* (4), 601–616.

McConnell, T. R., and Mortimer, K. P. *Sharing Authority Effectively*. San Francisco: Jossey-Bass, 1978.

Peterson, M. W. "Emerging Developments in Postsecondary Organization Theory and Research: Fragmentation or Integration?" *Educational Researcher*, 1985, *3* (14), 5–12.

Rokeach, M. *Beliefs, Attitudes and Values: A Theory of Organization and Change*. San Francisco: Jossey-Bass, 1968.

Senge, Peter M. *The Fifth Discipline: The Art and Practice of the Learning Organization*. New York: Doubleday Currency, 1990.

Schmidtlein, F. A. "Comprehensive and Incremental Decision Paradigms and Their Implications for Educational Planning." *Planning and Vocational Education*. Edited by G. H. Copa and J. Moss. New York: McGraw-Hill, 1983, 48–80.

Recent Selections

Alpert, D. "Performance and Paralysis: The Organizational Context of the American Research University." *Journal of Higher Education*, 1985, *56* (3), 241–251.

Clark, B. R. *The Higher Education System: Academic Organization in Cross-National Perspective*. Berkeley, CA: University of California Press, 1983.

March, J. G. "Emerging Developments in the Study of Organizations." *The Review of Higher Education*, 1982, *6* (1), 1–18.

Peterson, M. W., ed. *ASHE Reader on Organization and Governance in Higher Education*. 3rd ed. Lexington, MA: Ginn Press, 1986.

Schmidtlein, F. A. "Patterns of Institutional Governance and Decision Making Process." *Key Resources on Higher Education Governance, Management and Leadership*. Edited by M. W. Peterson and L. A. Mets. San Francisco: Jossey-Bass, 1987.

Classic Selections

Anthony, R. N., and Herzlinger, R. *Management Control in Non-Profit Organizations*. Homewood, IL: Irwin, 1975.

Baldridge, J. V.; Curtis, D. V.; Ecker, G.; and Riley, G. L. *Policy Making and Effective Leadership*. San Francisco: Jossey-Bass, 1978.

Beneviste, G. *The Politics of Expertise*. 2nd ed. Berkeley, CA: Glendessary, 1971.

Clark, B. R. "The Organizational Saga in Higher Education." *Administrative Science Quarterly*, 1972, *17* (2), 178–184.

Cohen, M. D.; March, J. G.; and Olsen, J. P. "A Garbage Can Model of Organizational Choice." *Administrative Science Quarterly*, 1972, *17*, 1–5.

Cyert, R. M. *Management of Non-Profit Organizations*. Boston: D. C. Heath, 1975.

Drucker, P. F. *Management: Tasks, Responsibilities, and Practices*. New York: Harper and Row, 1974.

————. *Age of Discontinuity*. New York: Harper & Row, 1969.

Forester, J. "Bounded Rationality and the Politics of Muddling Through." *Public Administration Review*, 1984, *44* (1), 23–31.

Havelock, R. G. *The Change Agent's Guide to Innovation in Education*. Englewood Cliffs, NJ: Educational Technology Publications, 1973.

Micek, S. S., ed. *Integrating Academic Planning and Budgeting in a Rapidly Changing Environment: Process and Technical Issues*. Boulder, CO: NCHEMS, 1980.

Rogers, E. M., and Shoemaker, F. F. *Communication of Innovations*. New York: Free Press, 1971.

Schmidtlein, F. A. "Decision Process Paradigms in Education." *Educational Researcher*, 1974, *3* (5), 4–11.

Simon, H. *Administrative Behavior*. 3rd ed. New York: Free Press, 1976.

Weick, K. E. "Educational Organizations as Loosely Coupled Systems." *Administrative Science Quarterly*, 1976, *21* (1), 1–19.

Critique of Planning

Over the years, a significant subset of the planning literature has evaluated and contrasted the potentials and limitations of planning practice, often arising from frustrations with the current state of the art. A number of excellent articles establishes the relative strengths and weaknesses of incrementalism and strategic decision making. This literature is essential to the planner for maintaining balanced perspectives between desired and realistic outcomes for current and future planning activities.

Critical Reading

Keller, G. *Academic Strategy: The Management Revolution in American Higher Education*. Baltimore: Johns Hopkins University Press, 1983.

Forester, J. "Bounded Rationality and the Politics of Muddling Through." *Public Administration Review*, 1984, *44*, 23–31.

Gray, D. H. "Uses and Misuses of Strategic Planning." *Harvard Business Review*, 1986, *64* (1), 89–97.

Meredith, Mark. "Strategic Planning and Management: A Survey of Practices and Benefits in Higher Education." Paper presented at the Association for Institutional Research Annual Forum, Portland, OR, 1985.

————; Lenning, Oscar; and Cope, Robert. "After Six Years, Does Strategic Planning Make Any Difference?" Paper prepared for the Association of International Research Forum, May 15–18, 1988, Phoenix, AZ.

————; Cope, Robert; and Lenning, Oscar. "Differentiating Bona Fide Strategic Planning from Other Planning." Technical paper. Boulder, CO: University of Colorado, ED 287 329, 1987.

Schmidtlein, Frank, and Milton, Toby. "Adapting Strategic Planning to Campus Realities. *New Directions for Institutional Research*, Number 67, Fall 1990.

Schnaars, Steven. *Megamistakes: Forecasting and the Myth of Rapid Technological Change*. New York: The Free Press, 1988.

Wildavsky, A. "If Planning is Everything, Maybe It's Nothing." *Policy Sciences*, 1973, 4 (2), 127–153.

Recent Selections

Baldridge, J. V., and Okimi, P. H. "Strategic Planning in Higher Education: New Tool—or New Gimmick?" *AAHE Bulletin*, 1982, 35 (2), 6 and 15–18.

Christensen, K. S. "Coping with Uncertainty in Planning." *Journal of the American Planning Association*, 1985, 51, 63–73.

Hayes, R. H. "Strategic Planning—Forward or Reverse?" *Harvard Business Review*, 1985, 111–119.

Hussein, Raef T. "A Critical Review of Strategic Planning Models." *Quarterly Review of Marketing*, Spring 1987, 8–13.

James, B. G. "Strategic Planning Under Fire." *Sloan Management Review*, 1984, 25 (4), 57–61.

Lindblom, C. E. "The Science of Muddling Through." *Public Administration Review*, 1959, 19 (2), 79–88.

Lindblom, C. E. "Still Muddling, Not Yet Through." *Public Administration Review*, 1979, 39 (6), 517–526.

Classic Selections

Boulding, K. "Reflections on Planning: The Value of Uncertainty." *Technology Review*, 1974, 77 (1), 8.

Clark, D. L. "In Consideration of Goal-Free Planning: The Failure of Traditional Planning Systems in Education." *Educational Administration Quarterly*, 1981, 17 (3), 46–60.

Enarson, H. L. "The Art of Planning." *Educational Record*, 1975, 56, 170–174.

Ewing, D. W. *The Human Side of Planning*. London: MacMillan Co., 1969.

Mandelbaum, S. J. "A Complete General Theory of Planning is Impossible." *Policy Sciences*, 1979, *11* (1), 59–71.

Millett, J. D. "Higher Education Management Versus Business Management." *Educational Record*, 1975, *56* (3), 170–174.

Moore, J. W. "Pragmatic Considerations in Academic Planning." *Planning for Higher Education*, 1976, *5* (6).

Poland, W., and Arns, R. G. "Characteristics of Successful Planning Activities." *Planning for Higher Education*, 1978, *7* (3), 1–6.

Richardson, R. C., and Gardner, D. E. "Avoiding Extremes in the Planning Continuum." *Journal of Higher Education*, 1983, *54* (2), 180–192.

Weidenbaum, M., and Rockwood, L. "Corporate Planning Versus Government Planning." *Public Interest*, Winter 1977, *46*, 59–72.

Strategic Planning/Strategic Management

Strategic planning is only one of the three types of planning—strategic, tactical, and operational. Within the literature on strategic planning is an excellent set of books, monographs, and articles which were selected to review the principles for strategic planning in general and to provide guidelines for applying them to higher education. A separate literature from public administration, political science, and policy studies provides an excellent grounding in the principles of policy. Special areas of emphasis include implementing policies, reconciling politics with science in policy analysis, and evaluating policies. Much of the work of policy analysis is inherently tactical in nature. However, it is critical in establishing strategy to understand the strategic implications of the requirements for policy formulation. Our selections provide such a focus.

Critical Reading

Bryson, J. M. *Strategic Planning for Public and Nonprofit Organizations*. San Francisco: Jossey-Bass, 1988.

Cope, Robert G. *Opportunity From Strength: Strategic Planning Clarified with Case Examples*. Washington, D.C.: ASHE-ERIC Higher Education Reports, No. 8, 1987.

Cope, R. G. *Strategic Planning, Management and Decision Making.* AAHE-ERIC/Higher Education Research Report No. 9. Washington, D.C.: American Association for Higher Education, 1981.

Hamel, Gary, and Prahalad, C. K. "Strategic Intent." *Harvard Business Review.* May-June, 1989, 63–76.

Lozier, G. Gregory, and Chittipeddi, K. "Issues Management in Strategic Planning." *Research in Higher Education,* 1986, 24, 3–14.

Marrus, Stephanie K. *Building the Strategic Plan.* New York: John Wiley & Sons, 1984.

Mitzberg, H. "Crafting Strategy." *Harvard Business Review,* 1987, 66–77.

_____, and McHugh, A. "Strategy Formation in an Adhocracy." *Administrative Science Quarterly,* 1985, *30,* 160–197.

_____, and Waters, J. A. "Strategies, Deliberate and Emergent." *Strategic Management Journal,* 1985, *6* (3), 257–272.

Ohmae, Kanichi. "Getting Back to Strategies." *Harvard Business Review,* 1988, *66* (6), 149.

Pennings, J., ed. *Organizational Strategy and Change: New Views on Formulating and Implementing Strategic Decisions.* San Francisco: Jossey-Bass, 1985.

Prahalad, C. K., and Hamel, Gary. "The Core Competence of the Corporation." *Harvard Business Review.* May-June, 1990, 79–91.

Schendel, D. E., and Hofer, C. W., eds. *Strategic Management: A New View of Business Policy and Planning.* Boston: Little, Brown, 1979.

Shirley, R. C. "Identifying the Levels of Strategy for a College or University." *Long Range Planning,* 1983, *16* (3), 92–98.

Steeples, Douglas W., ed. *Successful Strategic Planning: Case Studies, New Directions for Higher Education,* No. 64. San Francisco: Jossey-Bass, 1988.

Recent Selections

Below, Patrick J.; Morrisey, George L.; and Acomb, Betty L. *The Executive Guide to Strategic Planning*. San Francisco: Jossey-Bass, 1987.

Buhler-Miko, M. *A Trustee's Guide to Strategic Planning*. Washington, D.C.: Higher Education Strategic Planning Institute, 1985.

Chaffee, E. E. "Successful Strategic Management in Small Private Colleges." *Journal of Higher Education*, 1984, *55* (2), 212–241.

Cope, R. G. "A Contextual Model to Encompass the Strategic Planning Concept: Introducing a Newer Paradigm." *Planning for Higher Education*, 1985, *13* (3), 13–20.

Dutton, J. E., and Duncan, R. B. "The Creation of Momentum of Change Through The Process of Strategic Issue Diagnosis." *Strategic Management Journal*, 1987, *8*, 279–295.

Eadie, D. C. "Putting a Powerful Tool to Practical Use: The Application of Strategic Planning in the Public Sector." *Public Administration Review*, 1983, *43* (5), 447–452.

Eadie, D. C.; Ellison, N. M.; and Brown, G. C. "Incremental Strategic Planning: A Creative Adaptation." *Planning Review*, 1982, *10* (3), 10–15.

Lelong, D., and Shirley, R. C. "Planning: Identifying the Focal Points for Action." *Planning for Higher Education*, 1984, *12* (4), 1–7.

Lenning, O. T. "Successful Strategic Planning." Presentation at the Annual conference of the Christian College Coalition Academic Deans, Chicago, Illinois. February, 1987.

Lenz, R. T., and Lyles, M. "Managing Human Problems in Strategic Planning Systems." *Journal of Business Strategy*, 1986, *6* (4), 57–66.

_____. "Managing the Evolution of the Strategic Planning Process." *Business Horizons*, 1987, *30*.

Myran, Gundar A., ed. *Strategic Management in the Community College*. New Directions for Community Colleges, No. 44. San Francisco: Jossey-Bass, December 1983.

Classic Selections

Abell, D. F. *Defining the Business: The Starting Point of Strategic Planning*. Englewood Cliffs, NJ: Prentice-Hall, 1980.

Anshoff, R. *Strategic Management*. New York: John Wiley, 1979.

Baldridge, J. V. "Managerial Innovation—Rules for Successful Implementation." *Journal of Higher Education*, 1980, *51* (2), 117–134.

Bardach, E. *The Implementation Game: What Happens After A Bill Becomes Law*. Cambridge, MA: MIT Press, 1977.

Brewer, G. D. "Where the Twain Meet: Reconciling Science and Politics in Analysis." *Policy Sciences*, 1981, *13* (3), 269–279.

Doyle, P., and Lynch, J. "Long Range Planning for Universities." *Long Range Planning*, 1976, *9*.

Dror, Y. *Public Policymaking Reexamined*. 2nd ed. New Brunswick, NJ: Transaction Books, 1983.

Drucker, P. F. "The Deadly Sins in Public Administration." *Public Administration Review*, 1980, *25* (1), 103–106.

Fincher, C. "Planning Models and Paradigms in Higher Education." *Journal of Higher Education*, 1972.

Frances, C. "Apocalyptic vs. Strategic Planning." *Change*, 1980, *12* (5), 19 and 39–44.

Gluck, F. W.; Kaufman, S. P.; and Walleck, A. S. "Strategic Management for Competitive Advantage." *Harvard Business Review*, 1980, *58* (4), 154–161.

Haas, R. M. "Winning Acceptance for Institutional Research and Planning." In P. Jedamus and M. W. Peterson, *Improving Academic Management*. San Francisco: Jossey-Bass, 1980, 539–554.

Kotler, P., and Murphey, P. E. "Strategic Planning for Higher Education." *Journal of Higher Education*, 1981, *52* (5), 470–489.

Lelong, D. C., and Hinman, M. M. *Implementation of Formal Planning: Strategies for the Large University*. Ann Arbor, MI: Center for the Study of Higher Education, 1982.

Mayhew, L. B. *Surviving the Eighties: Strategies and Procedures for Solving Fiscal and Enrollment Problems*. San Francisco: Jossey-Bass, 1979.

Miles, R. E., and Cameron, K. *Coffin Nails and Corporate Strategies*. Englewood Cliffs, NJ: Prentice Hall, 1982.

Milgrom, Gail, and Sisam, Elizabeth. "Bridging the Gap Between Space Standards and Space Allocation: A Methodology." *Planning for Higher Education*, 1987, *16* (2), 31–42.

Palumbo, D. J. ed. "Symposium on Optimizing, Implementing and Evaluating Public Policy." *Policy Studies Journal*, 1980, *8* (3).

Paul, R. N.; Donovan, N. B.; and Taylor, J. W. "The Reality Gap in Strategic Planning." *Harvard Business Review*, 1978, *56* (3), 124–130.

Porter, R.; Oedel, P.; and Zemsky, R. "Adaptive Planning: The Role of Institution Specific Models." *Journal of Higher Education*, 1979, *56* (5), 586–601.

Poulton, N. L., ed. *Evaluation of Management and Planning Systems*. New Directions for Institutional Research No. 31. San Francisco: Jossey-Bass, 1981.

Pressman, J., and Wildavsky, A. *Implementation*. Berkeley, CA: University of California Press, 1973.

Quinn, J. B. "Strategic Goals: Process and Politics." *Sloan Management Review*, 1977, *19* (1), 21–37.

Quinn, J. B. "Strategic Change: Logical Incrementalism." *Sloan Management Review*, 1978, *20* (1), 7–21.

Quinn, J. B. "Managing Strategic Change." *Sloan Management Review*, 1980, *21* (4), 3–20.

Shirley, R. C. "Limiting the Scope of Strategy: A Decision Based Approach." *Academy of Management Review*, 1982, *7* (2), 262–268.

Wildavsky, A. *Speaking Truth to Power: The Art and Craft of Policy Analysis*. Boston: Little, Brown, 1979.

Wortman, M. S., Jr. "Strategic Management and Changing Leader-Follower Roles." *The Journal of Applied Behavioral Science*, 1982, *18* (3), 371–383.

Tactical Planning

Within the context of the general readings on planning and the context established by strategic planning, there exists a number of tactical planning areas, each with its own literature. For the planner whose particular organizational circumstance calls for a tactical approach, it makes sense to undertake some reading of the overall nature, history, context, and limitations of planning and strategic decision making, but to move quickly to the particular tactical area(s) of greatest interest.

There is substantial and varied literature supporting the various permutations of tactical planning. Much of this literature is time stamped by the nature of the challenges facing higher education of particular points in time—such as the retrenchment, management of decline, and resource-allocation emphasis of the late 1970s and early 1980s and the focus on productivity enhancement and cost control in the 1990s. We have selected a broad range of bibliographic citations for a variety of tactical planning topics.

Budgeting and Resource Allocation

In reviewing the budgetary and resource allocation process as a basic component of tactical planning, a number of outstanding books and articles emerges.

Critical Reading

Hearn, James C. "Strategy and Resources: Economic Issues in Strategic Planning and Management in Higher Education." Edited by J. C. Smart. *Handbook of Theory and Research in Higher Education*. New York: Agathon, 1988, 212–281.

Hyatt, J. A.; Shulman, C. H.; and Santiago, A. A. *Reallocation: Strategies for Effective Resource Management*. Washington, D.C.: National Association of College and University Business Officers, 1984.

Leslie, L. L. "Financial Management and Resource Allocation." *Key Resources on Higher Education Governance, Management and Leadership*. Edited by M. W. Peterson and L. A. Mets. San Francisco: Jossey-Bass, 1987.

Massey, William F. "Budget Decentralization at Stanford University." *Planning for Higher Education*, 1989, *18* (2).

Meisinger, Richard J., Jr. "Introduction to Special Issue on the Relationship Between Planning and Budgeting." *Planning for Higher Education*, 1989, *18* (2), 1–8.

Mingle, J. L., ed. *Management Flexibility and State Regulation in Higher Education*. Atlanta: Southern Regional Education Board, 1983.

Morrisey, George L.; Below, Patrick J.; and Acomb, Betty L. *The Executive Guide to Strategic Planning*. San Francisco: Jossey-Bass, 1988.

Schmidtlein, Frank A. "Why Linking Budgets to Plans Has Proven Difficult in Higher Education." *Planning for Higher Education*, 1989, *18* (2), 9–24.

Recent Selections

Anderson, Richard E., and Meyerson, Joel W., eds. *Financing Higher Education: Strategies After Tax Reform*. New Directions for Higher Education, No. 58. San Francisco: Jossey-Bass, 1987.

Gaffney, Eileen M. "Cost and Productivity Analysis for Higher Education: A Look at the Boston College Approach." *Planning for Higher Education*, 1987, *16* (1), 35–56.

Classic Selections

Caruthers, J. K., and Orwig, M. *Budgeting in Higher Education*. AAHE-ERIC Higher Education Research Report No. 3. Washington, D.C.: American Association for Higher Education, 1979.

Gillis, A. L. "Program Choice/Resource Compaction." *Planning for Higher Education*, 1982, *10* (3), 33–38.

Heim, P. "Management Systems and Budgeting Methodology: Do They Meet the Needs and Will They Work?" *NACUBO Studies in Management*, 1972, *2* (2).

Lyden, J. "The Budget Cycle as a Basis for Decision Making in Higher Education." *Planning for Higher Education*, 1975, *4* (5).

Massy, W. F. "Resource Management and Financial Equilibrium." *NACUBO Professional Files*, October 1975.

Orwig, M. D., and Caruthers, J. K. "Selecting Budget Strategies and Priorities." In P. Jedamus, M. W. Peterson, and Associates, *Improving Academic Management*. San Francisco: Jossey-Bass, 1980, 341–363.

Pfeffer, J., and Salancik, G. "Organizational Decision Making as a Political Process: The Case of a University Budget." *Administrative Science Quarterly*, 1974, *19* (1), 135–151.

Pfeffer, J., and Moore, W. L. "Power in University Budgeting: A Replication and Extension." *Administrative Science Quarterly*, 1980, *25* (4), 637–653.

Wildavsky, A. *The Politics of the Budgetary Process*. 3rd ed. Boston: Little, Brown, 1979.

Wildavsky, A. "A Budget for All Seasons?: Why the Traditional Budget Lasts." *Public Administration Review*, 1978, *38* (6), 501–509.

Retrenchment and the Management of Decline

A key component of both the strategic and resource allocation responses of the universities to the conditions of the 1980s has been the whole issue of responding to retrenchment and to what Boulding referred to as "The Management of Decline" in his article in *Change* in 1975.

Critical Reading

Baltes, Paula Choate. "Fiscal Stress and Implications for Planning." *Planning for Higher Education*, 1987, *16* (4), 3–18.

Hamlin, Alan, and Hungerford, Curtiss. "How Private Colleges Survive a Financial Crisis: Tools for Effective Planning and Management." *Planning for Higher Education*, 1988, *17* (2), 29–38.

Hardy, Cynthia. "Turnaround Strategies in Universities." *Planning for Higher Education*, 1987, *16* (1), 1–8.

Levine, C. H., and Rubin, I. *Fiscal Stress and Public Policy*. Beverly Hills, CA: Sage Publications, 1980.

Mingle, J. R. *The Challenges of Retrenchment*. San Francisco: Jossey-Bass, 1981.

Zammuto, R. F. "Managing Decline in American Higher Education." *Higher Education: Handbook of Theory and Research*, Vol. 2. Edited by J. C. Smart. New York: Agathon Press, 1986.

Zammuto, R. F., and Cameron, K. S. "Environmental Decline and Organizational Response." *Research in Organizational Behavior*, 1985, *7*, 223–262.

Recent Selections

Cameron, K. "Strategic Responses to Conditions of Decline." *Journal of Higher Education*, 1983, *54* (4), 359–380.

Hirschhorn, L., ed. *Cutting Back: Retrenchment and Redevelopment in Human and Community Services*. San Francisco: Jossey-Bass, 1983.

Jick, T. D., and Murray, V. V. "The Management of Hard Times: Budget Cutbacks in Public Sector Organizations." *Organization Studies*, 1982, *3*, 141–169.

Kerchner, C. T., and Schuster, J. H. "The Uses of Crisis: Taking the Tide at the Flood." *Review of Higher Education*, 1982, *5* (3), 121–141.

Petrie, H. G., and Alpert, D. "What is the Problem of Retrenchment in Higher Education?" *Journal of Management Studies*, 1983, *20*, 97–119.

Classic Selections

Behn, R. D. "Leadership for Cutback Management: The Use of Corporate Strategy." *Public Administration Review*, 1980, *40* (6), 613–620.

Boulding, K. "The Management of Decline." *Change*, 1975, *64*, 8–9.

Bowen, F. M., and Glenny, L. A. *Uncertainty in Public Higher Education: Responses to Stress at Ten California Colleges and Universities*. Sacramento: California Postsecondary Education Committee, 1980.

Cyert, R. M. "The Management of Universities of Constant or Decreasing Size." *Public Administration Review*, 1978, *38* (4), 344–349.

Levine, C. H., ed. *Managing Fiscal Stress*. Chatham, NJ: Chatham House, 1980.

Levine, C. H. "Organizational Decline and Cutback Management." *Public Administration Review*, 1978, *38* (4), 316–325.

Mortimer, K. P., and Tierney, M. L. *The Three R's of the Eighties: Reduction, Reallocation and Retrenchment*. AAHE/ERIC Higher Education Research Report No. 4. Washington, D.C.: American Association for Higher Education, 1979.

Rubin, I. "Universities in Stress: Decision Making Under Conditions of Reduced Resources." *Social Science Quarterly*, 1977, *58* (2), 242–254.

Smart, C., and Vertinsky, I. "Designs for Crisis Decision Units." *Administrative Science Quarterly*, 1977, 22 (4), 640–657.

Shaw, B. M.; Sandelands, L. E.; and Dutton, J. E. "Threat-Rigidity Effects in Organizational Behavior." *Administrative Science Quarterly*, 1981, *26* (4), 501–524.

Whetten, D. A. Organizational Responses to Scarcity: Exploring the Obstacles to Innovative Approaches to Retrenchment in Education." *Educational Administration Quarterly*, 1981, *17* (3), 80–97.

Program Review and Techniques of Evaluation

Evaluation of institutional programs is a critical tactical element. Evaluation can be summative and/or formative in nature depending upon the role evaluation has in the planning process. Program evaluation can also be directed at the unit, institution, and state levels. All of these perspectives are represented in the following citations.

Critical Reading

Barak, R. J. "Program Planning, Development and Evaluation." *Key Resources on Higher Education Governance, Management and Leadership*. Edited by M. W. Peterson and L. A. Mets. San Francisco: Jossey-Bass, 1987.

Barak, R. J. "The Role of Program Review in Strategic Planning." *AIR Professional File*. Tallahassee, FL: Association for Institutional Research, 1986.

_____. *Program Review in Higher Education: From Within and Without*. Boulder, CO: National Center for Higher Education Management Systems, 1982.

_____. "Seven Common Myths on Program Review." *Educational Record*, 1986, *67* (1), 52–54.

Conrad, C. F., and Wilson, R. F. *Academic Program Reviews: Institutional Approaches, Expectations, and Controversies*. ASHE-ERIC Higher Education Report No. 5. Washington, D.C.: Association for the Study of Higher Education, 1985.

Gilley, J. W.; Fulmer, K. A.; and Reithlingshoefer, S. J. *Searching for Academic Excellence*. New York: MacMillan/American Council for Education, 1986.

Steeples, D. *Institutional Revival: Case Histories*. San Francisco: Jossey-Bass, 1986.

Wilson, R. F., ed. *Designing Academic Program Reviews*. New Directions for Higher Education No. 37. San Francisco: Jossey-Bass, 1982.

Recent Selections

Adelman, C. *Assessment in American Higher Education*. Washington, D.C.: Office of Education Research and Improvement, U.S. Department of Education, 1986.

Barak, R. J., and Miller, R. I. "Rating Undergraduate Program Review at the State Level." *Educational Record*, 1986, *67* (2–3), 42–46.

Wilson, R. F., ed. "Critical Issues in Program Evaluation." *Review of Higher Education*, Winter 1984, *1*, 143–157.

Classic Selections

Anderson, S. B.; Ball, S.; Murphy, R. T.; and Associates. *Encyclopedia of Educational Evaluation*. San Francisco: Jossey-Bass, 1975.

Anderson, S. B., and Ball, S. *The Profession and Practice of Program Evaluation*. San Francisco: Jossey-Bass, 1978.

Arns, R. G., and Poland, W. "Changing the University Through Program Review." *Journal of Higher Education*, 1981, *51* (3), 268–284.

Barak, R. J., and Berdahl, R. O. *State-Level Academic Program Review*. Denver: Education Commission of the States, 1978.

Craven, E., ed. *Academic Program Evaluation*. New Directions for Institutional Research No. 27. San Francisco: Jossey-Bass, 1980.

Craven, E. Evaluating Program Performance. In P. Jedamus, M. W. Peterson, and Associates, *Improving Academic Management*. San Francisco: Jossey-Bass, 1980, 432–457.

Davis, C. K., and Dougherty, E. A. "Guidelines for Program Discontinuance." *Educational Record*, Winter 1979, *60* (1), 68–77.

Dressel, P. L. *Handbook of Academic Evaluation*. San Francisco: Jossey-Bass, 1976.

Feasley, C. E. *Program Evaluation*. AAHE/ERIC Higher Education Research Report No. 2. Washington, D.C.: American Association for Higher Education, 1980.

Franchak, S. J. *Using Education Results: Guidelines and Practice for Using Vocational Evaluation Effectively*. Columbus, Ohio: National Center for Research in Vocational Education, 1981.

Miller, R. I. *The Assessment of College Performance*. San Francisco: Jossey-Bass, 1979.

Munitz, B. "Examining Administrative Performance." In P. Jedamus, M. W. Peterson, and Associates, *Improving Academic Management*. San Francisco: Jossey-Bass, 1980, 478–494.

Patton, M. Q. *Utilization Focused Evaluation*. Beverly Hills, CA: Sage Publications, 1978.

Shirley, R. C., and Volkwein, J. F. "Establishing Academic Program Priorities." *Journal of Higher Education*, 1978, *49* (5), 472–488.

Warmbrod, C., and Persavich, J. J. *Post-Secondary Program Evaluation*. Columbus, Ohio: National Center for Research in Vocational Education, 1981.

Wildavsky, A. "The Self-Evaluating Organization." *Public Administration Review*, Sept/Oct 1972, *32* (5), 509–520.

Human Resources and Academic Planning

With the emergence of strategic planning, enrollment planning and management, and marketing in higher education, academic program planning has shifted in emphasis from program content to the needs of learners, the management of human and capital resources for program delivery, and the evaluation of program outcomes or "quality." The citations below represent a cross-section of these issues affecting academic program planning. Additional references relating to academic planning may be found under other headings in this bibliography.

Recent Selections

Birnbaum, Robert. "The Latent Organizational Functions of the Academic Senate: Why Senates Do Not Work but Will Not Go Away." *The Journal of Higher Education*, July/August 1989, *60* (4), 423–443.

Caret, Robert L.; Dumont, Richard G.; and Myrant, Mary-Ann. "Developing a Strategic Academic Staffing Plan Based Upon A Rationale of Institutional Reduction." *Planning for Higher Education*, 1987, *16* (2), 61–70.

Chan, Susy S. "Faculty Participation in Strategic Planning: Incentives and Strategies." *Planning for Higher Education*, 1987, *16* (2), 19–30.

Tack, M. W.; Rentz, A.; and Russell, R. L. "Strategic Planning for Academic Programs: A Strategy for Institutional Survival." *Planning for Higher Education*, 1984, *12* (4), 8–14.

Classic Selections

Blackburn, R. T. "Faculty Career Development: Theory and Practice." *Faculty Vitality and Institutional Productivity*. Edited by S. Clark and D. Lewis. New York: Teachers College Press, 1985, 55–85.

Fuller, B. "A Framework for Academic Planning." *Journal of Higher Education*, 1976, 47 (1), 65–77.

Heydinger, R. B. "Planning Academic Programs." In P. Jedamus, M. W. Peterson, and Associates, *Improving Academic Management*. San Francisco: Jossey-Bass, 1980, 304–326.

Jenny, H.; Heim, P.; and Hughes, G. *Another Challenge: Age 70 Retirement in Higher Education*. New York: TIAA-CREF, 1979.

Kells, H. R. "Academic Planning: An Analysis of Case Experiences in the Academic Setting." *Planning for Higher Education*, 1977, 6 (2), 2–9.

Patton, C. V. *Academia in Transition: Mid-Career Change or Early Retirement*. Cambridge, MA: Abt Associates, 1979.

Radner, R., and Kuh, C. *Preserving a Lost Generation: Policies to Assure a Steady Flow of Young Scholars Until the Year 2000*. Berkeley, CA: Carnegie Council on Policy Studies in Higher Education, 1978.

Zemsky, R.; Porter, R.; and Oedel, L. P. "Decentralized Planning: To Share Responsibility," *Educational Record*, 1978, 59 (3), 229–253.

Enrollment Planning and Management

The appearance of the term *enrollment management* merges the theory and practice of enrollment projection and forecasting, manpower supply and demand, marketing as applied to higher education, and the growing emphasis on recruiting and retention.

Critical Reading

Dolence, Michael G. "Evaluation Criteria for an Enrollment Management Program." *Planning for Higher Education*, 1989, 18 (1), 1–14.

Hossler, D. *Creating Effective Enrollment Management Systems*. New York: College Entrance Examination Board, 1987.

Litten, L. H.; Sullivan, D.; and Brodigan, D. L. *Applying Market Research in College Admissions*. New York: College Entrance Examination Board, 1983.

Zammuto, R. F. "Managing Declining Enrollments and Revenues." *Key Resources on Higher Education Governance, Management and Leadership*. Edited by M. W. Peterson and L. A. Mets. San Francisco: Jossey-Bass, 1987.

Zemsky, R. and Oedel, P. *The Structure of College Choice*. New York: College Entrance Examination Board, 1983.

Recent Selections

Baldridge, J. V.; Kemerer, F. R.; and Green, K.C. *The Enrollment Crisis: Factors, Actors, and Impacts*. Washington, D.C.: American Association for Higher Education, 1982.

Baldridge, J. V.; Kemerer, F. R.; and Green, K. C. *Strategies for Effective Enrollment Management*. Washington, D.C.: American Association of State Colleges and Universities, 1982.

Hossler, D. *Enrollment Management: An Integrated Approach*. New York: College Entrance Examination Board, 1984.

Hossler, D., ed. *Managing College Enrollments*. New Directions for Higher Education No. 53. San Francisco: Jossey-Bass, 1986.

Kotler, P., and Fox, K. *Strategic Marketing for Educational Institutions*. Englewood Cliffs, NJ: Prentice-Hall, 1985.

Classic Selections

Centra, J. A. *College Enrollment in the 1980's: Projections and Possibilities* New York: College Entrance Examination Board, 1978.

Grabowski, S. M. *Marketing in Higher Education*. AAHE/ERIC Higher Education Research Report No. 5. Washington, D.C.: American Association for Higher Education, 1981.

Ihlanfeldt, W. *Achieving Optimal Enrollments and Tuition Revenues*. San Francisco: Jossey-Bass, 1980.

Norris, D. M.; Lasher, W. F.; and Brandt, F. S. *Manpower Studies in Post-secondary Education.* AAHE/ERIC Higher Education Research Report No. 10. Washington, D.C.: American Association for Higher Education, 1977.

Kotler, P. *Marketing for Non-Profit Organizations.* Englewood Cliffs, NJ: Prentice-Hall, 1975.

Wing, P. "Forecasting Enrollment and Student Demographic Conditions." In P. Jedamus, M. W. Peterson, and Associates, *Improving Academic Management.* San Francisco: Jossey-Bass, 1980, 216–237.

Campus and Facilities Planning

In the literature, campus planning generally refers to the overall, integrative process of creating a campus master plan, which deals with the relationships between individual buildings and the campus as a whole. Facilities planning focuses upon the individual building and the systems which it contains.

Critical Reading

Brase, Wendell. "Integrating Physical Planning with Academic Planning." *Planning for Higher Education,* 1987, *16* (4), 41–52.

Clipson, C. W., and Johnson, R. E. "Integrated Approaches to Facilities Planning and Assessment." *Planning for Higher Education,* 1987, *15* (3), 12–22.

Dunn, John A., Jr. *Financial Planning Guidelines for Facility Renewal and Adaption.* Ann Arbor, MI: The Society for College and University Planning, December 1989.

Hyatt, James A. "Financing Facilities Renewal and Replacement." *Planning for Higher Education,* 1988, *17* (3), 33–42.

Milgrom, Gail, and Sisam, Elizabeth. "Bridging the Gap Between Space Standards and Space Allocation: A Methodology." *Planning for Higher Education,* 1987, *16* (2), 31–42.

Sensbach, Werner. "The University As A Real Estate Developer: A New Role for An Old Institution." *Planning for Higher Education,* 1988, *17* (1), 73–80.

Turner, P. V. *Campus: An American Planning Tradition*. Cambridge, MA: MIT Press, 1984.

Recent Selections

Beck, Mark W. "Campus Facility Site Selection and Matrix Evaluation of Weighted Alternatives: A Methodology." *Planning for Higher Education*, 1988, *17* (4), 33–40.

Brase, Wendell. "Design Criteria for Effective Classrooms." *Planning for Higher Education*, 1988, *17* (1), 81–92.

Dunn, John A., Jr. "Plant Upkeep and Financial Equilibrium: What Does It Take to Stay in Balance?" *Planning for Higher Education*, 1987, *16* (2), 11–18.

Wilson, L. S. "Planning for Excellence: The Capital Facilities Dilemma in the American Graduate School." *Planning for Higher Education*, 1987, *15* (1), 1–6.

Classic Selections

Bareither, H., and Schillinger, J. L. *University Space Planning*. Urbana, IL: University of Illinois Press, 1968.

Bullock, N.; Dickens, P.; and Steadman, P. *Theoretical Basis for University Planning*. Cambridge, England: Polyhedron Printers Ltd., 1968.

Danke, H. L.; Jones, D. P.; Mason, T. R.; and Romney, L. *Higher Education Facilities Planning and Management Models*. Boulder, CO: Western Interstate Commission on Higher Education, 1971.

Dober, R. P. *Campus Planning*. New York: Reinhold Publishing, 1964.

Hewitt, C. "Campus Renewal in the 1980's: The New Voyage of the Beagle." *Planning for Higher Education*, 1982, *11* (1), 14–24.

Kaiser, H. D., ed. *Managing Facilities More Effectively*. New Directions for Higher Education No. 30. San Francisco: Jossey-Bass, 1980.

Loomis, W., and Skeen, O. Evaluating the Adequacy of Campus Physical Facilities." *Planning for Higher Education*, 1977, *6* (3).

Mayer, F. "The Implementable Plan." *Planning for Higher Education,* Summer 1980, *8* (4), 1–6.

Regnier, J. H. "Improving the Utilization of Capital Facilities." In P. Jedamus, M. W. Peterson, and Associates, *Improving Academic Management.* San Francisco: Jossey-Bass, 1980, 392–405.

United Nations Educational Scientific and Cultural Organization. *Planning and Building Facilities for Higher Education.* New York: UNESCO Press/Dowd Hutchison and Ross, 1975.

Decision Support for Planning

One of the most highly developed bodies of literature is in the area of decision support for planning, which encompasses the use of information in planning, planning for technology, quantitative support of plans, and decision support systems. Our selection in this area covers a broad range of issues.

Critical Reading

David, G. B., and Holson, M. *Management Information Systems: Conceptual Foundations, Structure and Developments.* 2nd ed. New York: McGraw-Hill, 1985.

Hiltz, S. R., and Turoff, M. *The Network Nation: Human Communication via Computer.* Reading, MA: Addison-Wesley, 1978.

Hopkins, D. S. P., and Massy, W. F. *Planning Models for Colleges and Universities.* Stanford, CA: Stanford University Press, 1981.

Jarvinen, Galen. "Bringing the Factbook into the Electronic Age." *Planning for Higher Education,* 1988, *17* (4), 41–48.

Keen, P. F., and Scott-Morton, M. S. *Decision Support Systems: An Organizational Perspective.* Reading, MA: Addison-Wesley, 1978.

Quarterman, J. F., and Hoskins, J. C. "Notable Computer Networks." *Communications of the ACM,* 1986, *29* (10), 932–971.

Sapp, M. M. "Decision Support Systems for Strategic Planning." *CAUSE/ EFFECT,* *8* (5), 34–29.

Sheehan, B. S. "Decision Support: Applying Information, Computers and Telecommunications." *Key Resources on Higher Education Governance, Management and Leadership.* Edited by M. W. Peterson and L. A. Mets. San Francisco: Jossey-Bass, 1987.

Sprague, R. H., and Carlsen, E. D. *Building Effective Decision Support Systems.* Englewood Cliffs, NJ: Prentice-Hall, 1982.

Tetlow, W. L., ed. *Using Microcomputers for Planning and Management Support.* New Directions for Institutional Research No. 44. San Francisco: Jossey-Bass, 1984.

Recent Selections

Benjamin, R. I.; Rockart, J. F.; Scott-Morton, M.S.; and Wyman, J. "Information Technology: A Strategic Opportunity." *Sloan Management Review*, Spring 1984, *25* (3), 3–10.

Camillos, John C., and Lederer, A. L. "Corporate Strategy and the Design of Computerized Information Systems." *Sloan Management Review*, Spring 1985, *27* (3), 35–42.

Jones, D. P. *Data and Information for Executive Decisions in Higher Education.* Boulder, CO: National Center for Higher Education Management Systems, 1982.

Lucas, H. C. "A Corporate Strategy for the Control of Information Processing." *Sloan Management Review*, Spring 1982, 25–36.

McFarland, F. W.; McKenney, J. L.; and Pyburn, P. "The Information Archipelago–Plotting a Course." *Harvard Business Review*, 1983, *61* (1), 145–146.

McKenny, J. L., and McFarland, F. W. "The Information Archipelago–Maps and Bridges." *Harvard Business Review*, 1982, *60* (5), 109–119.

Rockart, J. F. "The Changing Role of the Information Systems Executive: A Critical Success Factors Perspective." *Sloan Management Review*, Fall 1982, *24* (1), 3–13.

Rockart, J. F., and Crescenzi, A. D. "Engaging Top Management in Information Technology." *Sloan Management Review*, Summer 1984, *25* (4), 3–16.

Rohrbaugh, J., and McCartt, T., eds. *Applying Decision Support Systems in Higher Education*. New Directions for Institutional Research No. 49. San Francisco: Jossey-Bass, 1986.

Sheehan, B. S., ed. *Information Technology: Innovations and Applications*. New Directions for Institutional Research No. 35. San Francisco: Jossey-Bass, 1982.

Sullivan, C. H. "Systems Planning in the Information Age." *Sloan Management Review*, Winter 1985, *27* (2), 3–12.

Classic Selections

Adams, C. R., et al. "Decision Making and Information Systems in Colleges." *Journal of Higher Education*, 1976, *57* (1), 33–49.

Ascher, W. "The Forecasting Potential of Complex Models." *Policy Sciences*, 1981, *13* (3), 247–267.

Buchanan, J. R., and Linowes, R. C. "Understanding Distributed Data Processing." *Harvard Business Review*, 1980, *58* (4), 143–153.

Buchanan, J. R., and Linowes, R. C. "Making Distributed Data Processing Work." *Harvard Business Review*, 1980, *58* (5), 143–161.

Carlson, E. D. "An Approach for Designing Decision Support Systems." *Data Base*, Winter 1980 (entire issue).

Feldman, M. S., and March, J. G. "Information in Organizations as Signal and Symbol." *Administrative Science Quarterly*, 1981, *26* (1), 171–186.

Hackman, J. D., and Libby, P. A. "Toward More Effective Strategic Planning: Annotated Readings About Planning, Human Information Processing and Decision Support Systems." *Planning for Higher Education*, 1981, *9* (4), 40–46.

Hopkins, D. S. P., and Schroeder, R. G., eds. *Applying Analytic Methods to Planning and Management*. New Directions for Institutional Research No. 13. San Francisco: Jossey-Bass, 1977.

Kantrow, A. M. "The Strategy Technology Connection." *Harvard Business Review*, 1980, *58* (4), 6–21.

Lawrence, G. B., and Service, A., eds. *Quantitative Approaches to Higher Education Management*. AAHE/ERIC Higher Education Research Report No. 4. Washington, D.C.: American Association for Higher Education, 1977.

Massy, W. F. "Reflections on the Application of a Decision Science Model to Higher Education." *Decision Sciences*, 1978, *9* (2), 362–369.

Sheehan, B. S. "Developing Effective Information Systems." In P. Jedamus, M. W. Peterson, and Associates, *Improving Academic Management*. San Francisco: Jossey-Bass, 1980, 510–538.

Ungson, G. R.; Braunstein, D.; and Hall, P. P. "Managerial Information Processing: A Research Review." *Administrative Science Quarterly*, March 1981.

Updegrove, D., ed. "Special Issue on Financial Planning Models: Benefits, Directions, Alternatives." *EDUCOM Bulletin*, Fall 1982.

New Directions in Planning

There are a number of new directions in planning which have special potential for future applications. In some cases these are old areas which are experiencing a renaissance or new level of importance based on emerging conditions. These areas will, over time, be absorbed into the mainstream of planning theory and practice.

Futures Techniques/Environmental Scanning

This area has been developing in the corporate world for a number of years. Through the efforts of James Morrison and other futurists, these techniques have been applied to higher education and are being utilized in a number of institutions. The literature is relatively well developed but is lacking in excellent case studies of successful application, which should appear in the next several years.

Critical Reading

Clagett, Craig A. "A Practical Guide to Environmental Scanning: Approaches, Sources, and Selected Techniques." *Planning for Higher Education*, 1988, *17* (2), 19–28.

Morrison, James L., and Mecca, Thomas V. "Managing Uncertainty: Environmental Analysis/Forecasting in Academic Planning." *Handbook of Theory and Research in Higher Education, 5.* Edited by John C. Smart. New York: Agathon Press, 1989, 354–390.

Callan, P. M., ed. *Environmental Scanning for Strategic Leadership.* New Directions for Institutional Research No. 52. San Francisco: Jossey-Bass, 1986.

Morrison, J. L.; Renfro, W. L.; and Boucher, W. I. *Futures Research and the Strategic Planning Process: Implications for Higher Education.* ASHE-ERIC/ Higher Education Research Report No. 9. Washington, D.C.: Association for the Study of Higher Education, 1984.

Morrison, J. L. "Establishing an Environmental Scanning/ Forecasting System to Augment College and University Planning." *Planning for Higher Education*, 1987, *15* (1), 7–22.

Recent Selections

Hearn, J. C., and Heydinger, R. B. "Scanning the University's External Environment–Objectives, Constraints, Possibilities." *Journal of Higher Education*, 1985, *56* (4), 419–445.

Lozier, G. G., and Chittipeddi, K. "Issues Management in Strategic Planning." *Research in Higher Education*, 1986, *24* (1), 3–14.

Morrison, J. L.; Renfro, W. L.; and Boucher, W. I., eds. *Applying Methods and Techniques of Futures Research.* New Directions for Institutional Research No. 39. San Francisco: Jossey-Bass, 1983.

Pflaum, A., and Delmont, T. "External Scanning, A Tool for Planners." *Journal of the American Planning Association*, 1987, *53* (1), 56–67.

Zentner, Rene D. "Scenarios, Past, Present and Future." *Long Range Planning*, 1982, *15* (3), 12–20.

Classic Selections

Harman, W. W. *An Incomplete Guide to the Future.* San Francisco: San Francisco Book Co., 1976.

Kirschling, W. R., and Huckfeldt, V. E. "Projecting Alternative Futures." In P. Jedamus, M. W. Peterson, and Associates, *Improving Academic Management.* San Francisco: Jossey-Bass, 1980, 200–215.

Competitive Advantage

The competitive advantage literature is well developed in the business sector. The concept has also been applied to higher education in the areas of student choice and institutional attractiveness and in case studies at institutions such as Carnegie Mellon, which have embraced the competitive advantage concept. What is lacking are examples of a broader set of applications of competitive advantage and descriptions of emerging institutional cultures in complex settings that weave together the results and interrelationships of a number of individual measures of the competitive study of particular programs. Our selections provide a grounding in the concepts of competitive advantage and some application to higher education.

Critical Reading

Ouichi, William. *The M-Form Society: How American Teamwork Can Recapture the Competitive Edge.* Reading, MA: Addison-Wesley, 1984.

Porter, M. E. *Competitive Advantage—Creating and Sustaining Superior Performance.* New York: Free Press, 1985.

Link, Albert, and Tassey, George. *Strategies for Technology-Based Competition.* Lexington, MA: Lexington Books, 1987.

Recent Selections

Benjamin, R. I.; Rockart, J. F.; Scott-Morton, M. S.; and Wyman, J. "Information Technology: A Strategic Opportunity." *Sloan Management Review,* 1984, 25 (3), 3–10.

Keen, P. *Competing in Time: Using Telecommunications for Competitive Advantage.* Cambridge, MA: Ballinger, 1987.

Ohmae, K. *The Mind of the Strategist: Business Planning for Competitive Advantage.* New York: Penguin Books, 1982.

Rowse, G. L., and Wing, P. "Assessing Competitive Structures in Higher Education." *Journal of Higher Education,* 1982, *53* (6), 656–686.

Partnerships Among Universities, Industry, and Government

The literature on new external relationships is well developed in establishing the historical antecedents and the current/future reasons for education, industry, and government joining forces in new ways. There are also reports identifying the kinds of initiatives that have worked in the past to establish research parks or other cooperative ventures. What is needed and will help greatly in future efforts are strategic evaluations describing which new organizational forms are working in the environment of the late 1980s and which of these will likely work in the future.

Critical Reading

Botkin, J., and Dimanescu, D. *The New Alliance — America's New R&D Consortia.* New York: Harper & Row, 1981.

Business-Higher Education Forum. *Beyond the Rhetoric: Evaluating University-Industry Cooperation in Research and Technology Exchange.* Vol. 1, The Case. Washington, D.C.: Author, 1988.

————. *Beyond the Rhetoric: Evaluating University-Industry Cooperation in Research and Technology Exchange.* Vol. 2, A Handbook. Washington, D.C.: Author, 1988.

Dimancescu, Dan, and Botkin, James. *The New Alliance: America's R&D Consortia.* Cambridge, MA: Ballinger, 1986.

Emmert, Mark A., and Crow, Michael M. "The Cooperative University Research Laboratory: Policy Implications for Higher Education." *The Journal of Higher Education,* July/August 1989, *60* (4) 408–422.

Fairweather, James S. "Academic Research and Instruction: The Industrial Connection." *The Journal of Higher Education,* July/August 1989, *60* (4), 388–407.

Matthews, J. B., and Norgaard, R. *Managing the Partnership Between Higher Education and Industry*. Boulder, CO: National Center for Higher Education Management Systems, 1984.

Norris, Donald M. "Partnerships Between Universities and Information Technology Vendors." *CAUSE/EFFECT*, Spring 1990, *13/ (1)*, 15–24.

Recent Selections

Association of American Universities. *Trends in Technology Transfer at Universities*. Washington, D.C.: Author, 1986.

Bernstein, Melvin H. *Higher Education and the State: New Linkages for Economic Development*. Washington, D.C.: National Institute for Work and Learning, ED 274 303, 1986.

Blumenthal, David; Gluck, Michael; Louis, Karen; Stoto, Michael; and Wise, David. "University-Industry Research Relationships in Biotechnology: Implications for the University." *Science*, 232 (4756), 1361–66.

Chmura, Thomas J. "The Higher Education-Economic Development Connection: Emerging Roles for Colleges and Universities." *Economic Development Commentary*, 1987, *11* (3), 1–7.

Dooris, Michael J. "Organizational Adaptation and the Commercialization of Research Universities." *Planning for Higher Education*. 1988, *17* (3), 21–32.

Fink, I. "The Role of Land and Facilities in Fostering Linkages Between Universities and High Technology Industries." *Planning for Higher Education*, 1985, *13* (3), 1–12.

Johnson, G. L. *The High Technology Connection: Academic Industrial Cooperation for Economic Growth*. ASHE-ERIC Higher Education Research Report No. 6. Washington, D.C.: Association for the Study of Higher Education, 1984.

Johnson, Robert F., and Edwards, Christopher G. *Entrepreneurial Science: New Links between Corporations, Universities, and Government*. Westport, CN: Greenwood Press, 1987.

Lee, C. A. "Research Park Development from a University Relation-ships Perspective." *Planning for Higher Education*, 1983, *12* (1), 33–40.

Public Policy Center, SRI International. *The Higher Education-Economic Development Connection: Emerging Roles for Public Colleges and Universities in a Changing Economy*. Washington, D.C.: American Association of State Colleges and Universities, 1986.

Effectiveness, Quality, and Outcomes

While the evaluation of effectiveness, quality, and outcomes has a long history, the centrality of these issues to higher education leadership has increased materially in recent years. External pressures to improve and measure quality and outcomes are encouraging institutions to face these issues more systematically and not to leave them to the complete discretion of each individual academic unit. Furthermore, literature is emerging on dealing with institutional effectiveness, which promises to be a critical area of focus for planners.

Critical Reading

Bergquist, William H., and Armstrong, Jack L. *Planning Effectively for Educational Quality*. San Francisco: Jossey-Bass, 1986.

Cameron, K. S. "A Study of Organizational Effectiveness and Its Predictors." *Management Science*, 1986, *32* (1), 87–112.

Conrad, C. F., and Blackburn, R. T. "Program Quality in Higher Education: A Review and Critique of Literature and Research." *Higher Education: Handbook of Theory and Research, Vol. 1*. New York: Agathon Press, 283–308.

Ewell, P. *The Self-Regarding Institution: Information for Excellence*. Boulder, CO: National Center for Higher Education Management Systems, 1984.

Litten, Larry H., and Hall, Alfred E. "In the Eyes of Our Beholders: Some Evidence on How High-School Students and Their Parents View Quality in Colleges." *Quality—Higher Education's Principal Challenge*. Edited by T. Stauffer. Washington, D.C.: American Council on Education, 1981.

McGuire, Joseph W.; Richman, Marie L.; Daly, Robert F.; and Jor-jani, Soheila. "The Efficient Production of 'Reputation' by Pres-tige Research Universities in the United States." *The Journal of Higher Education*, July/August 1988, *59* (4), 365–389.

Stauffer, T., ed. *Quality—Higher Education's Principal Challenge.* Washington, D.C.: American Council on Education, 1981.

Volkwein, J. Fredericks. "Changes in Quality among Public Univer-sities." *The Journal of Higher Education*, March/April 1989, *60* (2), 136–151.

Zammuto, R. F. "A Comparison of Multiple Constituency Models of Organizational Effectiveness." *Academy of Management Review*, 1984, *9* (4), 606–616.

Zammuto, R. F. *Assessing Organizational Effectiveness: System Change, Adaptation and Strategy.* Albany, NY: SUNY Albany Press, 1982.

Information Technology/Telecommunications

Information technology and telecommunications are critical instru-ments in reshaping the delivery of instruction, the conducting of research, and the administration of our colleges and universities. An excellent set of readings is emerging to guide our efforts in this direction.

Critical Reading

Digital Technology Task Force. *Report of the University Task Force on the Impact of Digital Technology on the Classroom Environment.* Blacksburg, VA: Virginia Polytechnic Institute and State Univer-sity, January 1989.

Green, Kenneth C., and Gilbert, Steven W., eds. *Making Computers Work for Administrators.* New Directions for Higher Education No. 62. San Francisco: Jossey-Bass, 1988.

King, Timothy D., and Lancaster, Ann-Marie. "How U.S. Colleges and Universities Can Confront Telecommunications Issues." *Plan-ning for Higher Education*, 1988, *17* (4), 13–26.

McCredie, John, ed. *Campus Computing Strategies.* Bedford, MA: Digital Equipment Corporation, 1983.

Penrod, James, and Dolence, Michael. "Strategic Planning for Information Resources Management." *CAUSE/EFFECT*, 1987, *10* (3), 10–17.

_____; Dolence, Michael G.; and Douglas, Judith V. *The Chief Information Officer in Higher Education*. Boulder, CO: CAUSE, Professional Paper Series No. 4, 1990.

Wood, Kenneth L. *Campus Networking Strategies*. Bedford, MA: Digital Press, 1988.

Recent Selections

Felder, Nathaniel L., and Britton, Thomas C. "Strategic Planning for Computing in a Multi-Campus Setting: A Case Study." *Planning for Higher Education*, 1987, *16* (4), 33–40.

Gilbert, Steven W., and Green, Kenneth C. "New Computing in Higher Education." *Change*, 1986, *18* (3), 33–50.

Faculty/Administrative Manpower and Workplace Issues

The academic workplace has reemerged as a critical issue in the 1990s. Possible faculty shortages, changes in faculty and administrative workload, and other considerations are drawing the planner's attention to these topics.

Critical Reading

Bowen, Howard R., and Schuster, Jack H. *American Professors: A National Resource Imperiled*. New York: Oxford University Press, 1986.

Clark, Burton R. "Planning for Excellence: The Condition of the Professoriate." *Planning for Higher Education*, 1987, *16* (1), 1–8.

Lozier, G. Gregory, and Dooris, Michael J. "Elimination of Mandatory Retirement: Anticipating Faculty Response." *Planning for Higher Education*, 1988, *17* (2), 1–14.

Massey, William F., and Zemsky, Robert. *The Dynamics of Academic Productivity*. Denver, CO: SHEEO, 1990.

_____. "The Administrative Office and the Academic Ratchet." Policy Perspectives. The Press Foundation, June 1990.

Changes in America and the University of the 21st Century

The changing American cityscape, the emergence of new metropolitan cities, and the emerging technologies are creating tremendous pressures for new types of universities. An intriguing literature on the universities of the 21st century is emerging.

Critical Reading

Verdun, John R., and Clark, Thomas A. *Distance Education: The Foundation of Effective Practice.* San Francisco: Jossey-Bass, 1991.

Commission on the University of The 21st Century, Commonwealth of Virginia. *The Case for Change,* 1990, Richmond, VA, 1.

Harkers, John. *New Heartland America's Flight Beyond the Suburbs and How It Is Changing Our Future.* New York: Times Books, 1986.

Norris, Donald M.; Delaney, Edward; and Billingsley, Kenneth. "America's New Cities." *Planning for Higher Education,* 1990, *19* (1), 1–8.

Recent Selections

Kinnick, Mary K., and Ricks, Mary F. "The Urban Public University in the United States: An Analysis of Change, 1977–1987." *Research in Higher Education,* 1990, *31* (1), 15–38.

Kott, Joseph. "Regional Economic Impact of Institutions of Higher Education." *Planning for Higher Eduction,* 1987, *16* (4), 19–32.

Rossini, Frederick A. "Transitions: The Synergistic Impacts of Major Technologies in the Twenty-second Century and Beyond." *Technological Forecasting and Social Change,* No. 36. Atlanta, GA: Elsevier Science Publishing Co., Inc., 1989, 217–222.

Public Sector/Nonprofit Management

Critical Readings

Axelrod, Nancy R. *The Chief Executive's Role in Developing the Non-profit Board.* Washington, D.C.: National Center for Nonprofit Boards, 1988.

Houle, Cyril. *Governing Boards: Their Nature and Nurture.* San Francisco: Jossey-Bass, 1989.

Kotler, Philip; Ferrell, O. C.; and Lamb, Charles. *Strategic Marketing for Nonprofit Organizations.* 3rd ed. Rev. Englewood Cliffs, NJ: Prentice Hall, 1987.

Norris, Donald M. *Market-Driven Management: Lessons Learned from 20 Successful Associations.* Washington, D.C.: ASAE, 1990.

Recent Selections

Bloom, C. "Strategic Planning in the Public Sector." *Journal of Planning Literature,* 1986, 1 (2), 253–259.

Barry, Bryan W. *Strategic Planning Workbook for Nonprofit Organizations.* St. Paul, MN: Amherst W. Wilder Foundation, 1986.

Park, Dabney. *Strategic Planning and the Nonprofit Board.* Washington, D.C.: National Center for Nonprofit Boards, 1990.

7

Sources of Information and Professional Organizations

Specialized Associations of Interest

Planners seem compelled to group together to discuss their field. The following address list of professional associations dealing with planning may be of assistance to the new planner seeking information on membership, services, and publications.

1. Society for College and University Planning
   2026M School of Education Building
   The University of Michigan
   Ann Arbor, Michigan 48109-1259

2. Association for Institutional Research
   314 Stone Building
   Florida State University
   Tallahassee, Florida 32306

3. Planning Forum
   5500 College Corner Pike
   PO Box 70
   Oxford, Ohio 45056

4. Issues Management Association
   105A Old Long Ridge Road
   Stamford, Connecticut 06903

5. World Future Society
   4916 St. Elmo Avenue
   Bethesda, Maryland 20814-5089

6. American Association for Higher Education
   One Dupont Circle, Suite 600
   Washington, D.C. 20036

7. Amercian Institute of Architects
   1735 New York Avenue, N. W.
   Washington, D.C. 20006

8. Council of Educational Facilities Planners-International
   1060 Carmack Road, Suite 160
   Columbus, Ohio 43210-1002

Publications

SCUP publishes a newsletter and a journal, *Planning for Higher Education*, while the Association for Institutional Research (AIR) publishes a newsletter and a journal, *Research in Higher Education*. Jossey-Bass sponsors a series of more comprehensive monographs on issues pertaining to higher education planning entitled *New Directions in Institutional Research*. The American Association for Higher Education (AAHE) also concerns itself with planning along with other areas of interest and publishes a series of research reports annually, some of which deal with planning issues. The Association for the Study of Higher Education (ASHE) also encourages research and a publication series that can have planning-related material. An interesting international journal is *The International Journal of Institutional Management in Higher Education*.

As a cross- and interdisciplinary endeavor, planning articles can appear in a wide variety of publications. Other journals which regularly provide articles on planning and policy analysis include the following:

Change
Harvard Business Review
Journal of the American Institute of Planners
Long Range Planning
Academy of Management Review
Management Science
Policy Sciences Journal
Administrative Science Quarterly
Public Administration Review
The Political Science Quarterly
Sloan Management Review
NACUBO Professional File